Information Technology

Authors
Paul Reynolds
Tom Charnley

Series editor
Alan Brewerton

A level

Every effort has been made to trace copyright holders and to obtain their permission for the use of copyright material. The authors and publishers will gladly receive information enabling them to rectify any error or omission in subsequent editions.

First published 1998
Reprinted 2000

Letts Educational, Schools and Colleges Division, 9–15 Aldine Street, London W12 8AW
Tel. 0208 740 2270
Fax 0208 740 2280

Text © Paul Reynolds and Tom Charnley 1998

Editorial, design and production by Hart McLeod, Cambridge

All our rights reserved. No part of this publication may be reproduced, stored in a retrieval system, or transmitted, in any form or by any means, electronic, mechanical, photocopying, recording or otherwise, without prior permission of Letts Educational.

British Library Cataloguing-in-Publication Data

A CIP record for this book is available from the British Library

ISBN 1 84085 108 2

Printed and bound in Great Britain

Letts Educational Ltd, a division of Granada Learning Ltd. Part of the Granada Media Group.

Contents

Introduction 4
Core topic 1 Nature and types of software 5
Core topic 2 Peripherals 8
   Extension topic 1 Bitmaps and OCR
Core topic 3 User interfaces/terminology 13
   Extension topic 2 Human–computer interface
Core topic 4 Networks and distributed systems 18
   Extension topic 3 Repeaters, bridges and backbones
   Extension topic 4 OSI: The open system interconnection model
   Extension topic 5 Distribution
Core topic 5 Role of communication systems 24
   Extension topic 6 Packet switching systems
Core topic 6 Portability of data 27
Core topic 7 Security of data 29
Core topic 8 Software capabilities 32
   Extension topic 7 Software to support specialist applications
Core topic 9 Upgradability 38
Core topic 10 Reliability of software 40
Core topic 11 Configurability of hard/software 42
Core topic 12 Modes of processing 44
Core topic 13 Relational databases 47
Core topic 14 Verification/validation 52
Core topic 15 Data, information and knowledge 55
   Extension topic 8 Information
   Extension topic 9 Data
Core topic 16 Effective presentation 61
Extension topic 10 Organisational structure 62
Extension topic 11 Information systems and organisations 64
Extension topic 12 Definition of a management information system 66
Extension topic 13 The development and life cycle of an information system 67
Extension topic 14 Success or failure of a management information system 69
Extension topic 15 Information flow 71
Extension topic 16 Personnel and information systems 73
Extension topic 17 Developments within management information systems 74
Extension topic 18 Corporate information systems strategy 77
Extension topic 19 Expert systems and artificial intelligence 79
Core topic 17 Capabilities and limitations of IT systems 82
Extension topic 20 The management of change 83
Extension topic 21 Audit requirements 85
Extension topic 22 Disaster recovery management 88
Core topic 18 Security, the Data Protection Act and EU Directives 91
Extension topic 23 Legal aspects 97
Core topic 19 IT and the professional 99
Extension topic 24 Training 101
Extension topic 25 User support 103
Extension topic 26 Project management and effective IT teams 105
Core topic 20 Role of IT and its social impact 107

Answers 112
Index 127

Introduction

This revision guide focuses on the A/S and A level IT syllabuses recently introduced by the NEAB.

The guide is divided into sections headed 'Core' and 'Extension', which cover syllabus items appropriate for the A/S and the full A level, respectively. The guide does not discuss the requirements for course work, only the four written examination sections.

This guide must be read in conjunction with the current examination syllabus in order to see how the notes fit the syllabus requirements. Where appropriate we have included some past examination questions, along with their 'official' answers, as well as a range of questions of our own which are designed to help you direct the notes towards specific answers.

A few case studies are included to show IT solutions at work – the type of thing you could include to help support your written answers. There are plenty more examples in the weekly and monthly computer/IT press – look out for them and make a little note of their substance. Examples show you are aware of developments in you subject and lend authenticity to your answers.

Finally
This guide is not a substitute for class notes and discussions – it is an aid to revision and assumes you have already done your background preparation!

Core topic 1

Nature and types of software

If you can kick it, it's hardware!

Difference between hardware and software

Hardware is the physical parts of a computer system such as screens, printers, disk drives etc.

Software is the programs that control the use of the hardware. As they cannot be 'touched' they are called software.

Different types of software

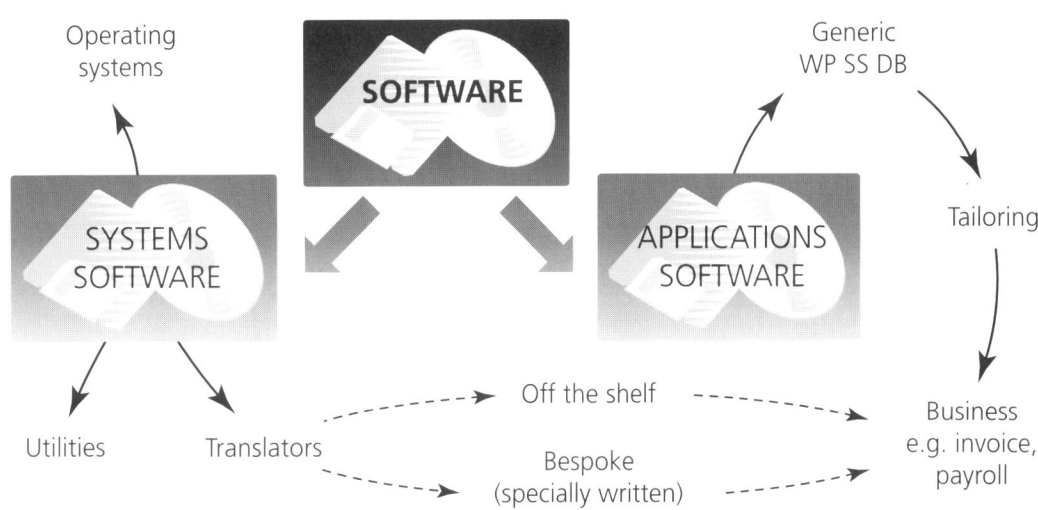

Figure 1 Different types of software

The above diagram shows that software can be classed into two broad types, **systems software** and **applications software**.

The bold line shows how we use IT in problem solving, the dotted line shows the conventional computing approach.

In order to solve a problem, there are three main strategies:

- buy a ready-made, **off-the-shelf** solution
- pay to have a programmer/analyst solve your problem by **writing a special program** for you
- pay to have a package **tailored** to solve your problem.

There are advantages and disadvantages to each approach:

	Advantages	Disadvantages
Off-the-shelf packages	Available, tested, cheap due to volume production. Large customer base	Might do too much, or not enough.
Bespoke solutions	Fit problem exactly.	Take time to be written and tested, can be inflexible. Costly due to small volume.
Tailoring of generic packages	Package may already be used, little training required for use. Easier to prototype.	Time taken (but faster than bespoke), testing.

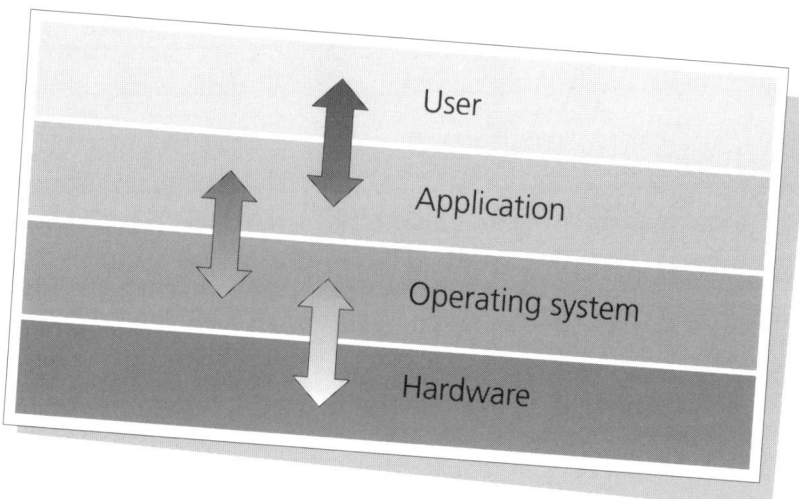

Figure 2 How the user, software and hardware communicate

System software

System software is programs that 'look after' the computer and allow you to use it.

Operating systems

- control the hardware
- allow the user and applications to communicate with the hardware.

Without an operating system, the computer is useless. The main functions of an operating system are

- **allocating main memory** to programs and their data without getting them mixed up
- looking after **backing storage allocation**, ensuring files don't get mixed up
- **communicating** with peripherals such as keyboards, printers etc. when they need attention.

Examples of operating systems are MS-DOS, UNIX or WINDOWS 95.

Utilities are:

- programs like file management programs, disk formatters, disk repairers, virus protection programs etc.
- often written by third parties
- used to extend the usability of the operating system.

Translators

- are used to **translate programs** written in computer languages like Visual Basic, COBOL, FORTRAN, C, into **binary machine code**. (That's the only code a computer can run, all programs eventually have to be translated to it.)
- allow a programmer to solve a problem using the '**language of the problem**' then have it translated into machine code, rather than have to program in machine code directly. It's a bit like saying 'knit 1 pearl 2' etc. in a knitting pattern, which is the 'language of solving knitting problems', rather than having to explain exactly what the needles have to do to knit an entire jumper.

Applications software

Applications software is programs designed to solve users' problems.

> Do not say word-processor, spreadsheets or databases when asked for examples of business packages, use these.

Typical business applications are:

- invoicing (billing customers and receiving payments)
- payroll (paying your staff) and stock control.

The familiar word-processing and spreadsheet packages are called **generic (general purpose)** or productivity packages. (During your projects you will tailor these packages to solve business problems.)

In general terms -

- a word-processor handles **text and graphics**
- a spreadsheet is used for **processing numbers**
- a database is used for the **storage, retrieval and processing of data**.

Integrated packages vs suites of programs

An integrated package

- has limited word-processing, database, spreadsheet, graphics and communication modules
- is designed so that a single data file can be manipulated by these modules
- is designed from scratch to do this task. e.g. MS Works.

Discrete packages (not integrated) need a separate file for each function giving:

- much duplication of data
- loss of **integrity**, i.e. correctness, if the files get out of step with each other.

A suite, such as MS Office, contains the more complex big brothers of these modules, each being a package in its own right, e.g. Excel, Word. These have been rewritten to some extent to allow the passing of data between them.

An integrated package tends to be cheaper, but does not have as many features.

Core topic 1 Nature and types of software

Questions

1. Describe three functions of an operating system.

2. Explain the term **utility program** with reference to one you have used.

3. How does solving problems using traditional languages compare to the tailoring of packages?

4. Compare and contrast solving a business problem using off-the-shelf as opposed to bespoke solutions.

5. Distinguish, with examples, the difference between hardware and software.

6. Name three common business applications.

7. What are the advantages of an integrated package compared to using discrete packages?

8. Explain, with the aid of a diagram, how an operating system helps to insulate the user from the hardware.

9. Explain the term 'tailoring' and what advantages this may have in solving IT problems in a business situation.

Core topic 2

Peripherals

Peripheral means 'around the edge'.

Peripherals are the devices found 'around the edge' of the central processing unit (CPU) – often called the processor.

There are four broad classes: input, output, storage and communication devices.

A device to transfer data from human to machine understandable form.

Input devices

Keyboard

- Most people are familiar with the QWERTY keyboard, but there are also specialist keypads such as the one-handed writer and the concept keyboard, where sections of a pad are overlaid e.g. tills.

Mouse

- Usually 2 or 3 buttons.
- Works by the rotation of the ball being 'sensed' in X and Y directions.
- Some can be infrared with no cable.
- A tracker ball is used on some notepads, acting like an upside-down mouse.
- Also 'finger mice' or track pads, where you have a special window and the pressure of your fingertip moves the pointer as you move your finger.

Joystick/game pad

- Often used in games, the more sophisticated sense the speed of movement as well as direction.

Touch screen

- A special layer senses where screen is pressed, or infrared beams detect the finger.
- Often used without keyboard.

Scanner

- Optical device that senses light reflected from an image as a series of dots.
- Resolution is how many dots across and down.

Extension topic 1

Bitmaps and OCR

A scanned image, in pixel format is called a bitmap as each pixel is represented by a number of bits (binary digit, 0 or 1).

- If the image is **monochrome**, each pixel can be **black or white only**, so a single bit can be used to represent the pixel.
- If **two bits** per pixel are used, **four** colours can be used for the four possible patterns e.g. BLACK=00, BLUE=01 GREEN=11 and RED=10.
- For **three bits**, **eight colours**, represented by the possible codes 000 001 010 011 100 101 110 111 can be used.
- Eight bits per pixel (1 byte per pixel) allows 256 colours and 16 bit gives 65526 possible colours.

If a pixel on the screen is stored as a code using 16 bits (two bytes):

- a typical picture with resolution 640x480 consists of 307200 pixels, which needs 614400 bytes, or approx. 600 Kbytes of memory.

OCR (optical character recognition) is used to recognise text in a bitmap image.

- By attempting to **recognise the patterns of letters** in the picture, it is possible to save the data as a text file.

Bar code reader

- Another optical device that works on the reflected light principle, the differing thickness of lines and spaces being used to store data.
- Bar codes are difficult to read by humans.
- Examples are grocery bar codes storing product data and book bar codes storing ISBN.

Grocery bar codes don't contain price of goods.

In an exam, I once saw a student use a tube of sweets as an example.

Speech recognition

- Attempts to analyse the patterns of waves produced by speech into words.
- Requires a great deal of processing power.
- Difficult to use in noisy environments where the input can be distorted by background noise or in quiet environments (e.g. a library) where use of speech interface is intrusive on others.
- Has to be able to cope with languages, dialects and day-to-day changes in voice patterns, e.g. colds.
- Often the software has to learn by the user speaking pre-defined sentences.
- The better software learns as you correct it and so becomes more accurate. Useful for sight-impaired people.

MICR (Magnetic ink character reader/recognition)

- Special characters are printed using magnetic ink.
- When passed through a magnetic field the patterns can subsequently be read.
- Has the advantage of being human readable as well.
- Common use on bank cheques.
- No use in magnetic environments e.g. label on a metal can.

OMR (Optical mark reader)

- Uses reflected light to sense whether a mark has been made or not.
- Used on lottery tickets and multiple choice exam answer papers.

Output devices

Machine to human understandable form.

Printers

Impact

Dot matrix

- Uses a row of pins e.g. 9 or 24 pins, to strike ribbon onto paper.
- Builds up characters in a vertical manner, can also be used for graphics.
- Slow (100 characters per second) and noisy, but cheap.
- Used in supermarket checkouts.

Useful for multi-part stationery (carbon copies).

Line

- Although now mainly superseded by fast laser printers, they are still used with multi-part stationery.
- A line of text is built up from a band rotating next to the ribbon with the letters on it.
- There is a set of hammers, one for each place in the line.
- These are triggered when the letter is over the correct place in the line of text.

Thermal

- Similar to dot matrix but pins are heated and no ribbon is involved.
- Uses special paper which reacts to the heated pins.
- Quieter than dot matrix.

Ink-jet

- Ink is fired from small jets onto paper using electrostatic charge.
- Quick and better quality than dot-matrix.
- Colour versions give very good results.
- Used mainly in home/small office.
- Cheap to buy, expensive to run as ink cartridges are relatively expensive.
- About three pages per minute.

Bubble jet

- Similar to ink-jet, but ink is heated in small chamber and bubble forms which 'bursts' the ink onto the page.

Laser

- Uses a laser to write a pixel image line by line onto an electrostatic drum.
- This rolls in an ink bath and picks up ink where it is charged, rolled onto paper, then fused by heated rollers (ink has glue in it).
- Expensive to buy, cheap to run compared to ink-jet. Colour is becoming available but expensive.
- Used in offices and schools.
- About six pages per minute.

Fast laser

- Churns out multiple copies as fast as a photocopier.
- In fact the two technologies are converging, with the newest digital photocopiers being a scanner and fast laser combined.

Colour laser

- Still very expensive to buy and run.

Plotter

- used in computer aided design/drafting (CAD).
- Pens are used and either the pen moves in small X and Y directions on a flat bed (X-Y plotter), or the paper is moved under the pen in one direction, while the pen moves in the other (Drum plotter).
- Slow, but good accuracy and different coloured pens can be used.

COM (Computer output on microfilm)

- The resulting microfilm is compact and easily transportable, and is read using a microfilm reader.

- Many libraries use these to store archive material.
- CD ROM is starting to replace this to some extent.

Sound

- Sound patterns can be sampled and stored for later playback.
- But this takes a lot of memory, e.g. a three-minute stereo song where the waveform is sampled at CD quality (44,000 times a second) takes about 40 Mbyte of space.
- This is because each sample is made up of a 16 bit binary number (2 bytes of information).
- If fewer samples are taken, or fewer bits used for each sample, the quality goes down.
- Sound can also be generated using phonetic techniques to recreate words.
- Can sound very computer-like, e.g. talking petrol pumps.

Storage devices

Store data in machine understandable form.

Main store

- Main store in the computer is RAM (Random Access Memory).
- This is where your programs are normally run, but it is volatile (i.e. content is lost when switched off), so non-volatile secondary or backing storage such as disks are needed.
- ROM (Read Only Memory) is used on some computers to store programs, e.g. games cartridges, as these too are non-volatile.
- Other possibilities are Programmable ROM (PROM), Erasable PROM (EPROM), Electrically Eraseable PROM (EEPROM sometimes pronounced 'e-squared ROM'), and Electrically Alterable ROM (EAROM).

Backing storage

Magnetic media (data stored using magnetic techniques)

Magnetic strip

- The strip on the back of a credit card can hold a few tens of characters only, e.g. the sort code and account number on a bank card.

Magnetic tape

- Used mainly for security copies (back-ups) and are called tape streamers.
- The cartridges look a bit like small video cassettes.
- Larger reel-to-reel systems are not much used nowadays, except on mainframes.

Floppy disk

- The 1.44 Mbyte floppy is familiar, but the new generation can hold 100Mbytes or more.
- Disks have to be formatted to lay out magnetic markers.
- Data is stored in concentric (circular) tracks, marked into sectors.
- Slow compared to hard disks.
- Portable, can be used to transport data easily and cheaply.

Hard disk

Getting bigger and faster, typically 2–4 Gbyte. Usually non-removable and can fail if knocked about.

> When data is carried to another location it can be thought of as a secondary input device, but is not a true input device as the data is stored in machine understandable form.

Optical media

WORM CD-ROM (Write Once, Read Many Compact Disk Read Only Memory)

- Laser burns pits into disk, read by a low power laser as 0s and 1s, as light is reflected or not.
- Can store about 650 Mbytes, access times getting faster, 24 speed common, but speed of rotation limited by the strength of disk.
- Usually has only one laser read head and one surface, whereas a hard disk has many surfaces, e.g. 10, and many read/write heads per surface.
- So a hard disk can find a track more quickly, although once located, the transfer rate is about the same. Blank disks can cost as little as £1.

WR CD Rom

- Re-writeable CDs cost more, but can be re-used.

Communication devices

Networks

Typical devices are network cards – see section on local area networks, page 18.

Modems

See section on wide area networks, page 21.

Core topic 2 Peripherals

1 Describe a keyboard other than a conventional QWERTY keyboard and give a use for it.

2 When might a touch screen be a useful input device?

3 Describe three input devices that use optical techniques and give a use for each.

4 'The development of speech input and output will make keyboards obsolete.' Do you agree? Give reasons.

5 Explain the terms OMR MICR and OCR and give a use for each.

6 Justify, with reasons, a printer suitable for a) the home, b) a card cash machine, c) a small office, d) a gas company.

7 Name three magnetic storage devices and compare each in turn with CD-ROM storage.

8 Name and describe an output device suitable for the design department of a house building company.

9 Why is the 1.44 Mbyte floppy disk still a popular storage medium, even though it has small capacity?

Extension topic 1 Bitmaps and OCR

1 A scanner is to be used to scan an old photograph. Explain the different size of files you would get if the picture was colour instead of black and white.

Core topic 3: User interfaces/terminology

Not in security situations – who would design a screen that says 'Enter password to access secret files'!

The development of human–computer interfaces

The term HCI (human–computer interface) means 'where the computer and humans meet'. It is also taken to mean how the humans and computers communicate.

User interfaces are normally designed to be efficient and user-friendly. Often the skills of ergonomists and psychologists as well as the IT specialist are used in their design.

Command line interface

The user has to type in commands on a Command Line Interface, such as MS-DOS.

Figure 3

Users became expert in all the commands and found it fast once they had learned them, but it was **difficult for a first-time user**.

Figure 4 A full screen menu

Full screen menus

- These were developed to help users, especially new users. All options are shown on the screen. Choosing an option will usually bring up a screen of further options, until the required one is found.
- This can get annoying for expert users who don't want to have to go through the many levels of menu screens. In order to overcome this, shortcut keys or **macros** are used.
- Shortcut keys are defined by the program and could be, e.g. CTRL+P for print, or F1 key for help.
- Macros record any sequence of keystrokes needed to navigate the menu to get to a required option. The macro can then be played back by the user by pressing a combination of a couple of keys.
- Macros have since been incorporated into many packages and, in their most sophisticated state, they can be edited and have control structures such as loops and branches, much like programming languages, and can be assigned to mouse events as well as keys. Programmable keys are often called Soft Keys.
- Dedicated keys are keys like Shift, Home, Print Screen, End etc.

USER INTERFACES/TERMINOLOGY 13

Menu trees

The way you can navigate a menu system can be shown in a tree diagram:

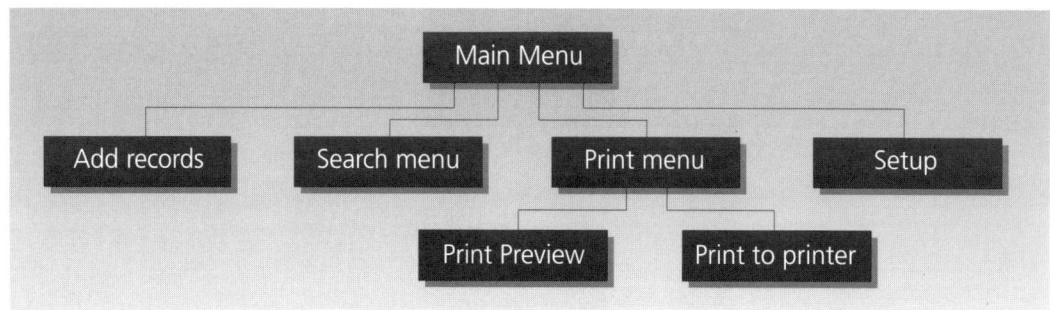

Figure 5 Menu tree

WIMP interface

- Invented in the 1980s for Apple Macintosh computers.
- An even simpler and more intuitive way of working than full screen menus.
- It stands for Windows, Icons, Menus and Pointers (or some say Windows, Icons Mouse and Pull-down menus).
- Also sometimes called a **graphical user interface (GUI)**.
- You should be most familiar with this type of intuitive interface and its use of dialogue boxes where you point, click and fill in boxes, e.g.

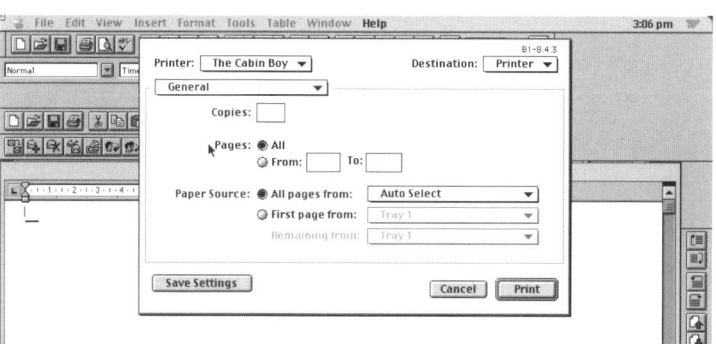

Figure 6 WIMP dialogue box

Advantages over the full screen menus

- You can drop the menus down when desired.
- It leaves the work area uncluttered.

'Families' of software, e.g. Microsoft, came to adopt similar interfaces.
This gave many advantages:

- increased speed of learning as skills were **transferable**
- ease of use
- confidence building in users when trying new packages
- increased range of tasks solvable by experienced users (again transferable skills, solve it in one package, similar in another)
- greater range of software accessible to average user.

Disadvantages:

- It **takes a lot of processor time** and memory to achieve this WIMP type of interface.
- A command line or simple menu system **will always work faster**.
- An expert user will want to use keys, e.g. a typist doesn't want to have to move his/her hands from the keyboard to use the mouse, so often shortcut keys are provided that perform the same function as mouse clicks.

Speech input

Speech input is becoming more common with programs like Voice Assist being given away with sound cards. This software allows you to control a WIMP interface by voice.

Dictation programs are also becoming more widely available, as the speed and memory of computers increase. These allow you to translate speech into text.

There are drawbacks:

- noisy environments
- speech impediments may prevent the computer recognising speech sounds correctly.

Speech output

This is where words are spoken by the computer. It can be used to help blind users, etc.

The words are formed from either

- pre-recorded words which are stored in a dictionary
- or by forming the words from phonemes.

Like phonetics in spelling.

Natural dialog

- This can be **typed or spoken**.
- It is a modern extension of the command line interface.
- Users learn to use almost natural English sentences to control the computer, e.g. 'Show sales for March to December as a pie chart'.
- The advantage is that once the user has learned the restricted grammar allowed, it is flexible in use.
- But the user can be fooled into thinking that the computer is more intelligent than it actually is!

*Don't just think this is **spoken** dialogue – it can be keyed in.*

Extension topic 2

Human–computer interface

> The HCI of a computer-based information system is one of its most important components. It tries to match the most efficient ways in which a human can work with the requirements of the system.

There are two major levels of operation when considering an HCI:

The physical level – which covers how the user interacts with the system

- screen is always visible – not facing window, causing user to lose track of the image
- space required by user is adequate – notes can be rested easily, knee and elbow room considered
- design of mouse and keyboard is ergonomically acceptable
- furniture is adjustable to suit each user therefore maximising comfort
- ventilation/temperature control is comfortable for users
- colour schemes suited to environment – gentle on the eye, not garish and distracting causing screen views to be lost in the background.

The psychological or conceptual level – which covers how the user thinks about the system

- user-friendly interface
- help available for novice users
- shortcuts for expert users

- makes use of human long-term memory to maximise efficiency
- the system operates in the way for which it was designed (functionality)
- the design helps to overcome some people's fear of machines (technophobia).

These levels determine different approaches in developing the HCI. The HCI defines not only what the system will do but also what the user can do, and aims to bring the two together in such a way that the user appears to operate the system in a natural and obvious (intuitive) way, with little reference to help pages.

The book entitled *Design of Man–Computer Dialogue* by J. Martin (Prentice Hall, 1973) contains criteria for a 'good' HCI.

- Speed of response – one-tenth of a second appears to be the goal of systems designers. Expectations have risen in line with the developments in technology.
- Ease of use – the user should not have to spend much time in learning the basic operating tools. It should have an intuitive feel.
- Limited memorisation of commands – the user should not have to remember long command sequences in order to operate the system – a lessening chore for regular users, but a distinct barrier for casual and novice users!
- On-line assistance. The interface should be designed in such a way that the user doesn't have to refer to manuals, rather to on-line help which is part of the application, and which could also assist in time of error. The system should respond with a clear explanation of the problem and how the user might solve it.

Communicating with machines

Factors to be considered when developing a human–computer interface might include:

- command/menu structures
- screen design
- nature of error messages
- availability of help
- user friendliness
- ease of learning.

The resource implications of sophisticated HCIs – which might include voice recognition and playback – are quite considerable.

Interface designers are making use of the power available on the desktop whilst manufacturers are adding to that power.

- For example: voice recognition and command systems have been around for a number of years, but the processing power has been with large organisations such as universities and government research centres. Developments including high speed processors and cheap storage – RAM and disks – have now brought these facilities into offices.

As users see what is possible they become more demanding both of themselves and the support facilities. There is greater demand for

- memory
- backing store
- processor functionality
- time/speed.

Each development has a cost implication for the company, which is not likely to go away. Maintenance and improvements have to be built into the budget.

Quite often it is necessary to develop a specialist HCI, maybe to control a dangerous process or to help someone with a disability. None of these developments come for nothing. Costs may be counted in terms of assessment, programming and implementation plus any upgrade costs to equipment.

For example:

- On-line help availability leads to increased need for backing store.
- Complexity of interface/multiplicity of menu routes adds to size of resultant code thus increased IAS demands. (IAS=Intermediate Access Store. The more complex the program, the greater amount of RAM it requires in order to run successfully. Old versions of Windows were 'happy' with 4mb but the newer versions such as Windows 95 require 16mb of RAM for really efficient operation.)
- use of and changes to GUI result in increased IAS demands.
- need for multi-tasking (ability to switch between applications/tasks) leads to processor functionality overhead (making the processor do more things) leading to slower responses or complete failure as the demands placed upon the processor reach capacity.
- faster searching of help file means processor speed overhead.

Questions

Core topic 3 User interfaces/terminology

1 Describe the human computer interface you would expect to find on the following situations:
   a) A nursery (pre-reader) program
   b) A graphic design program
   c) A control program for a robot (e.g. Turtle).

2 What are the advantages and disadvantages of a command line interface compared to a full screen menu system?

3 Explain the term **macro** in the context of a human-computer interface.

4 What are the advantages and disadvantages of speech interfaces?

5 Explain, with the aid of a diagram, a menu tree.

6 In a WIMP interface, what is a dialogue box? Describe one you have used.

7 Explain, giving reasons, which features of a human–computer interface you would expect to be used by a) a new user, b) an expert.

Extension topic 2 Human–computer interface

1 Ergonomics is the study of the relationship between the human and his environment. One area this relates to in IT is the design of hardware for ease of use, e.g. mice. Can you think how it could be applied to give an efficient and easy to use WIMP interface?

2 Describe a natural or free-form dialogue interface.

3 In the early 1980s, there were few common features between the interfaces for the popular packages. What advantages would a new user have nowadays?

Core topic 4: Networks and distributed systems

The keywords to remember in networking are Sharing and Communication.

A network is a number of computers, physically remote, connected by a communication channel.

You can have two types, local area networks, which cost nothing to run after initial installation, and wide areas networks, which have installation, connection and sometimes usage charges.

Communication methods

- In analogue transmission, the signal sent varies continually and **mimics the pattern** of the source, e.g. a sound wave.
- A digital signal is prepared by sampling the analogue signal, i.e. reading its **value** many thousands of times per second.
- These values are rounded up to a number of pre-set values.
- These values are then stored or transmitted as binary pulse trains.

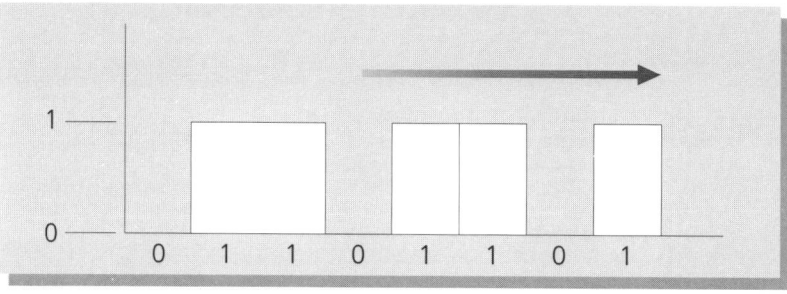

Figure 7 Pulse train

Serial transmission

Serial: data bits sent one after another.

- The pulse train is sent down a **single** wire
- along with bits for error correction and starting and stop bits.

Parallel transmission

Parallel: side by side.

- Several bits, usually 8 or 16, each sent down **its own wire at the same time**.
- Transmission is faster.
- Signal wires for end-to-end synchronisation are also used.
- Advantages – faster.
- Disadvantages – more wiring costs, problems with electrical interference between wires means that short distances only are practical.

Local area networks

LANs are on ONE site, e.g. a school (which may have many buildings).

Advantages:

These allow the **sharing** of
- peripherals, e.g. printers
- software, e.g. word-processor packages
- data files, e.g. student timetables
- also allow communication between stations.

Disadvantages include:

- the cost of installing the network
- the problems with network crashes affecting all users
- increased problems with security of data (see page 29)

Sometimes a local area network has a **file server** where the data and application files are stored. This machine is dedicated to this task, i.e. it can't be used for anything else.

Another way is to have a **peer-to-peer** network, where each station has its own application files. This cuts down on network traffic, but is harder for a network manager to upkeep as new software has to be installed on all machines.

(A new way of working using network computers, developed for the Internet WAN, but which can also be used in Intranet LANs, is to store all programs and data remotely. The Java applets (mini programs) or data files are retrieved when necessary. The computers are called 'thin clients' as opposed to PC's 'thick'.)

The **topology**, or layout, of the network can affect its price and performance and resistance to crashes.

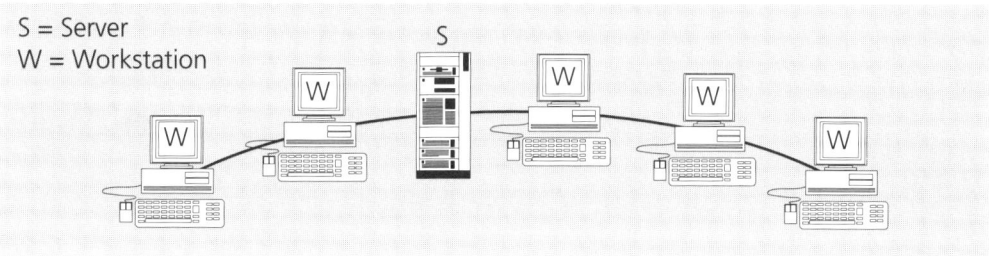

*Figure 8 **Bus** (or multi-drop) network topology: cheap, simple cabling, prone to crashes and clashes (two stations trying to talk at same time).*

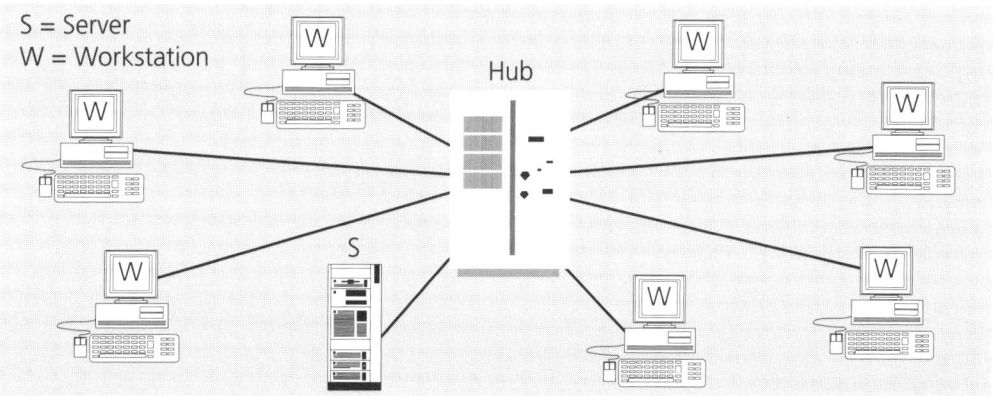

*Figure 9 **Star** network: expensive to cable, fast, more resistant to faults as, if a single limb is affected, the others work normally. Needs a central hub to connect the computers together.*

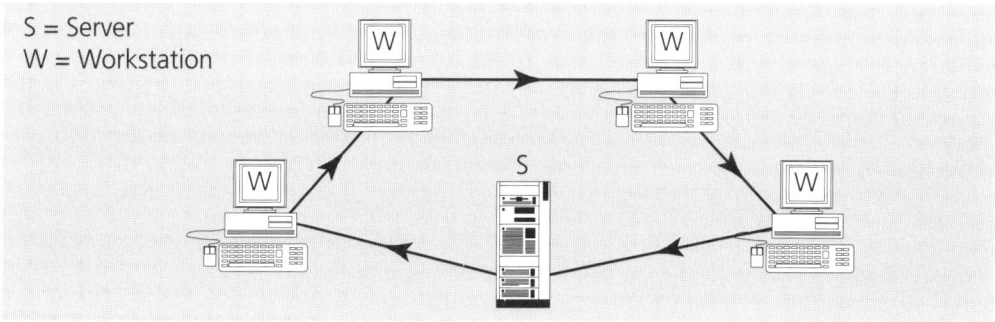

*Figure 10 **Ring** topology: slower, uses a 'free' circulating token that station seizes and inserts its message and destination. Token is 'released' on reply, thus not allowing clashes. Prone to cable faults, takes more cable than bus, less than star.*

Pass the parcel.

NETWORKS AND DISTRIBUTED SYSTEMS

Extension topic 3

Repeaters, bridges and backbones

- A common type of network is Ethernet, which can be cabled as a bus or star network.
- There is a maximum distance for a section or segment of cable.
- Beyond this length a **repeater** (a form of amplifier that regenerates the signal) must be used.
- This type of network allows clashes to occur. If there are many machines on the network, clashes occur frequently.
- This slows the service down as the computers are clashing, waiting, trying again then clashing again.
- To try to stop this the network can be broken down into smaller sections or clash domains, with a bridge between the sections.
- The **bridge** allows a machine on one side of the bridge to talk to one on the other side but, in normal use, all traffic between the stations on one side of the bridge is isolated and not seen by machines on the other.
- In a server system, this means a server is needed on each side of the bridge, otherwise there would be no benefit as all machines would still have to talk to the server, causing clashes.
- A **backbone** can be found in a bus or star network.
- This main segment then feeds other segments via hubs, repeaters or bridges.

Extension topic 4

OSI: The open system interconnection model

For interconnecting networks.

In an attempt to standardise the way networks are designed so that different types of networks using different protocols can more easily be interconnected, the OSI model was developed.

- The purpose of OSI is to provide an architecture which defines communication tasks.
- The basic idea of OSI is that computer communication for any given task is **too complex** to be considered as a complete entity.
- Instead it should be considered as a set of layers, each successive layer built on top of a lower layer and using its facilities.
- The internals of each layer are of no importance in the OSI model.
- What is important is the **overall function of the layer** and its interface to higher and lower layers.
- By standardising these layers and their interfaces, OSI attempts to allow a user to alter techniques used in a given layer without affecting the appearance of the overall system to the user.
- This will allow the user to switch manufacturers without having to sacrifice his system.

OSI uses a seven layer model.

- The user's application sits above the top layer and uses its facilities.
- Underneath the bottom layer is some underlying communication system.

To try to explain the seven levels of the OSI model I will use the analogy of a telephone conversation, rather than computers talking:

7 *Application layer*

In this layer I'm having a phone conversation, but to set it up I had to dial, which needed the services of the next layer:

6 *Presentation*

My telephone is an old one with pulse dialling but this layer transforms them into a common format that the telephone system understands, i.e. tone dialling, which was used by the next level to:

5 *Session*

connect me to another phone. In the session I can use the next layer to:

4 *Transport*

Transport speech both ways. To do this without a crossed line I need the services of the next layer:

3 *Network*

The connection is made using phone numbers and routes information between them. To make sure my voice is OK we use the next layer:

2 *Data link*

Which makes sure no information is lost due to errors. It in turn uses the next layer:

1 *Physical*

It provides mechanical, electrical, functional and procedural means to activate, maintain and deactivate physical connection, in other words – the physical phone network.

During a conversation between computers, each layer of **computer one** is 'talking' to its counterpart layer at **computer two**, controlling the communications for that layer, and allowing data to pass up and down the layers at each side:

> The OSI was developed to allow networks of different types to be interconnected, by agreeing to standard interfaces between the layers.

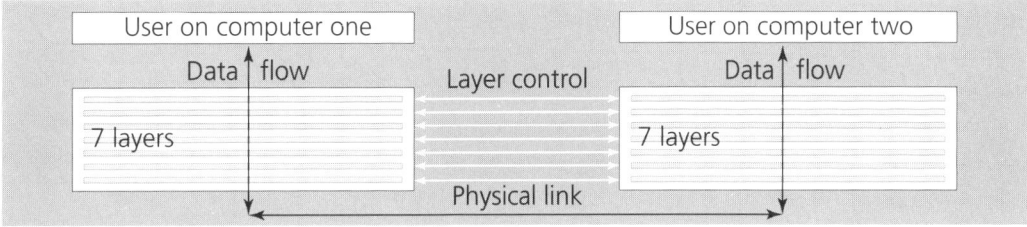

Figure 11 OSI model

The same sort of approach is used in PC design and manufacture, where a video card or CPU can be swapped as long as it has a compatible interface.

Wide area networks

> WANs are computers connected on different sites.

Connect computers which are **physically remote** by a communications system, usually BT.

- To use ordinary telephone lines, a modem is required, to change the **on/off clicks** of a digital signal (which can't pass down phone lines) to **tone/no tone** of an analogue signal.
- The analogue signal is designed to pass down a phone line as it is speech frequency.
- At the other end another modem is used to convert the analogue signal back to digital.

The Internet

What is it?

- It's a WAN!
- It's a collection of computers around the globe, allowing users access to data, most of which is free.
- The process of accessing data from remote sites is TELEMATICS/INFORMATICS.
- To surf the net, you need a connection into the system.

- Use a modem and a phone line to your local Internet Service Provider.
- Pay around £100 a year plus local call charges. Some advertisers offer free connection.
- The connection speed is around 3000 characters (bytes) a second, which sounds fast, until I say a hard disk can transfer data at around 500,000 bytes per second.
- To get a faster connection pay £1000+ for ISDN link, but still only 11,000 characters per second!
- Internet connection offered by the cable companies will be much faster, but the cable companies have been slow getting this off the ground!
- Other features are e-mail and newsgroups.
- These are provided by Internet Service Providers and third parties such as yahoo.com and allow us to send mail to others with an e-mail address and receive mail to our mailbox.
- Note, the mailbox is on another computer, usually belonging to the ISP, so we can receive mail even when our own computer is switched off.

Advantages:

- e-mail
- access to billions of pieces of information world-wide
- search engines to help sift information
- chat with others.

Disadvantages

- time taken to connect
- time taken to search
- time taken to download information to local machine
- pornography and other criminal activities
- viruses.

Network speeds

- LANs work at about 1Mbyte-10Mbyte per second transfer rate, but this has to be shared amongst the users on line at that moment.
- One user would get 1Mbyte/sec, but 10 users only 100Kbytes per second, and 100 simultaneous users would get 10K/sec.
- WANs using a modem have a theoretical limit of about 5K/sec, as the limiting factor is that the phone line is designed for speech.
- **Compression** is often used to try to speed up transmission (e.g. send A5 instead of AAAAA).
- **ISDN** (integrated services digital network) connections are much more expensive but allow greater throughput of data.
- A phone line currently has a limit of about 56,000 characters per second (slower than a floppy disk), an ISDN connection can be four times faster than this.
- Again this throughput has to be shared amongst the number of simultaneous users.
- The latest **DSL** (digital subscriber line) technologies will allow for speeds up to 1 Mbyte/second over ordinary phone lines.
- A **gateway** is a computer or device that connects LANs to WANs, or WANs to WANs. (The LANs and WANs can be of similar or dissimilar types.)
- **Fibre optic cables** will allow speeds comparable to hard disk speeds, 1–10Mbyte/sec.
- Optical fibres are robust and less prone to electrical interference.
- Optical fibres are more secure as they are much more difficult to intercept.

Extension topic 5

Distribution

Distributed systems mean not only the **distribution of processing power** in the form of networks as opposed to centralised mainframe installations, but also the possibility of **distributing the data** and the control over that data.

A database management system (**DBMS**), with distributed processing, is where the data tables are held centrally and muti-access is allowed from remote sites.

- Data is transferred to remote site.
- Data is processed at the remote site.

A more modern approach is **client/server** technology, i.e. a dedicated database server where:

- requests only are passed from the client (remote site) to the server
- the server processes the data
- the answer only is returned
- so transmission of large data files is avoided.

A distributed database management system (DDBMS) is where:

- the data is stored on different sites in a physical sense
- the database is viewed as a logical whole
- when the database is opened, the whereabouts of the data is 'transparent' to the user – they just see a set of tables, even though the tables might be stored in different locations
- the advantage is that tables can be owned and processed locally and then the changes seen by all the others
- disadvantages include the possible problems with communication, including speed, and the complexity of the whole system.

Questions

Core topic 4 Networks and distributed systems

1 What are the advantages and disadvantages of networking computers as opposed to stand-alone computers?

2 A company is increasing the size of its server-based local area network. Explain how the company can guard against its slowing down.

3 Explain the difference between an Intranet and the Internet.

4 Draw and label diagrams showing three network topologies and explain the advantages and disadvantages of each.

5 A business has a head office building and ten sites in different parts of the country. How can a WAN help to run its business?

6 Compare the speed of LANs and WANs.

Extension topic 3 Repeaters, bridges and backbones

1 Explain the different uses of a repeater, hub and bridge.

Extension topic 4 The OSI model

1 What is the OSI model and which problem is it meant to solve?

Extension topic 5 Distribution

1 Explain how the term distribution can refer to processing or data.

NETWORKS AND DISTRIBUTED SYSTEMS

Core topic 5

Role of communication systems

Don't forget: Comms systems DON'T have to include computers.

A communication system can be:

- **SIMPLEX** (one way), such as TV or CEEFAX (BBC's VIEWDATA system)
- **half-duplex** such as CB radio (both directions but not at the same time)
- **DUPLEX** such as telephones (both directions at once)
- one to one – such as telephone – or one to many – such as television.
- Some are many to many, e.g. video conferencing.

Telephones – can be analogue or digital

In an analogue telephone system:
- you talk into handset and carbon granules are compressed
- change in resistance creates **changing current**
- this passes down wires into speaker of other telephone.

In a digital telephone system:
- the changes in resistance are **sampled as values**
- these values are passed down the line.

Features of telephone systems

- One to one, or you can have teleconferences.
- Recent features include call waiting, call announce, call back, messaging systems, etc. and touch-tone enquiry systems such as direct banking by phone.
- Automatic queuing systems on answer.
- Mobile phones have advantages and disadvantages, e.g. convenience vs cost, reception range, annoyance to others.

Television

- Can be terrestrial broadcast, cable or satellite.
- Analog at the moment: picture formed by three electron beams moving across and down TV screen and exciting phosphor dots.
- Digital, where pixels are used rather than line by line, shortly to be introduced in UK.
- One to many.
- Cable are hoping to introduce a 'video and music on demand' system.

Viewdata (e.g. CEEFAX, Oracle)

- Textual data sent using the top few free 'lines' of conventional TV.
- Limited amount of data, broadcast page by page continuously.
- (What will happen when digital arrives?)
- Simplex. Free (once you've bought a teletext television!).

Viewdata (e.g. Prestel)

- Forerunner of Internet.
- Used mainly by holiday companies/airlines.
- BT network, three computers.
- Uses CEEFAX-like pages and graphics but two-way.
- Local call charges.

Fax

- Uses a telephone line.
- Passes a scanned black and white image to another fax machine.
- Expensive if long distance.
- One to one.
- Poor quality.
- Not accepted as legal document.

Telex

- Another global network.
- Based on text from teletypewriters.
- In decline.
- Accepted as legal document.

Telegraph

- Not used in UK now.
- Based on Morse code.
- Replaced by telemessage.

Internet super highways, see WANs, page 21

E-mail

- Sending messages.
- Allows one to many, checking if received, forwarding, storing, replying.
- Fast, inexpensive (local call charges and Internet Provider subscription).

E-fax

- Uses a scanner to scan pictures, or simply sends word-processed document from computer via modem to fax machine at other end.

Informatics/Telematics

- Gathering and organising data at a distance, e.g. Internet browsers.

Extension topic 6

Packet switching systems

Instead of connecting the circuit first and then exchanging messages (i.e. circuit switching – very expensive if long distance), a local connection is made to a network of computer nodes that can **route packets of information** via the least congested path.

- **Messages** are broken down into **packets**.
- These are sent around the system which has intelligent nodes.
- Some packets can arrive before others as they are routed differently according to traffic.
- Packet contains address of who to, address of who from, data, error correction data and packet number (so the message can be rebuilt).

- The forerunner of packet switching was message switching, but this required the nodes to store the message before forwarding it and this takes time and storage space.
- Packet switching is **faster** than waiting for a gap to get all message down.
- If any errors occur, then **only the affected packets** need to be retransmitted, not the whole message.
- It is also **more secure**, as packets are difficult to intercept as they can go via different routes.

Questions

Core topic 5 Role of communication systems

1 How would the introduction of an internal e-mail system in a large office block change the way people work?

2 Compare and contrast the use of e-mail with both telephone and fax.

3 Explain how **informatics** or **telematics** has increased with the advent of the Internet and readily available search engines.

4 Explain the advantages of e-mail over traditional mail.

5 Explain, with examples, the terms **simplex**, **half-duplex** and **duplex**.

Extension topic 6 Packet switching systems

1 In packet switching, what is a packet and what does it contain? Why is packet switching used more often than circuit switching?

2 Why is it preferable to send the same e-mail to a number of different sites using packet switching, rather than circuit switching?

3 Why are sequence numbers needed in packet switching?

Core topic 6

Portability of data

Not just moving, but being useable at end of journey.

Portability means that data can be moved or carried and be useable at the end of its journey.

It can be stored on a floppy disk, CD-ROM, tape or a laptop hard disk and carried, or it can be electronically transmitted from one place to another.

When it arrives at the other place, there could be problems, depending on how the data is to be used.

It might want to be used between:

- different applications on the same machine, e.g. a word-processing package and spreadsheet
- the same type of machine running a different package, e.g. Word and AmiPro
- different type of machine, e.g. PC and MAC. You may have come across this problem yourself.
- **Data is valuable**, time is invested in creating it, so you don't want to have to retype it, you want it to be reusable.
- Manufacturers normally provide you with **export and import filters** to achieve this.

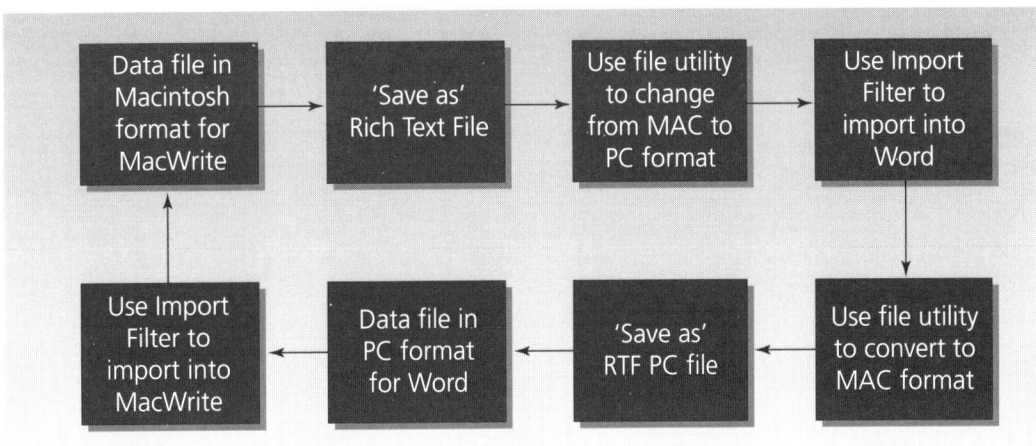

Figure 12 Using import and export filters

- If the correct filter is not available, by using a lower level filter such as raw text, the main body of the text can be transferred, but the formatting such as bold, indent, etc. is lost.

This topic is also related to upgradability and the different versions of software. See pages 38 and 7.

- In order to transfer data safely, **standard formats** have been agreed internationally, e.g. **ASCII** (American Standard Code for Information Interchange).
- Before these standards were agreed, translator programs had to be written to transfer data from one system to another.
- As the number of systems by different manufacturers rose, so the number of possible permutations and the number of corresponding translator programs grew, until they all got together to agree on a formal standard.
- Some standards arise from the popularity of a particular package and are called *de facto* standards, e.g. Word format for word-processors.

You might ask why do other software and hardware manufacturers support these standards? Just consider the problems of going it alone: your package can't import anyone else's, so if you take your file anywhere else it will be useless. So no-one who, say, works in two places, e.g. home and college, will buy it.

Questions

Core topic 6 Portability of data

1. Your word-processing file that you created at home won't work on the school computers. Give three possible reasons for this, excluding hardware faults.

2. Explain the difference between a *de facto* standard and a formal standard.

3. Explain the use of import and export filters.

4. ASCII stands for American Standard Code for Information Interchange, but why did this standard become necessary?

5. A company is using a database package that has no export facilities and they wish to change to another package that has no import facilities. What options do they have in order to make this changeover?

6. A company wishes to move from one operating system to another. What are the implications for the transfer of their data?

7. At home your word-processor can only save work as its own type or as a text file. What would be the implications of this if you wished to take some work into school where a different word processing package is used?

Core topic 7

Deliberate or accidental damage.

Security of data

Data and information is valuable and it must be kept secure from:

- **deliberate corruption**
- **accidental corruption.**

Accidental corruption

Screen prompts such as 'Are you really sure you want to delete this', or locking file to 'read only' can help, but the best way to guard against natural disasters such as flood or fire, is to make copies and keep them safely off site.

Back-up copies

There are many types of back-ups and which you choose for a particular installation will depend upon money available and also **how critical the loss of data** would be. After a back-up has been performed, it is important to remove the copy to a **safe location**, usually off site, although a fire-proof cabinet is often used. This will allow the system to be recovered in the event of a disaster. (See section on disaster recovery, page 88.)

Different types of back-up:

File copy

- Simply copy the file to another medium, e.g. floppy disk.
- File must be small enough to fit.
- Simple, but any changes in between copies will be lost.

Incremental back-up

This is useful for data that is relatively static, i.e. doesn't change much, for example a desktop computer that stores its data files on a network.
  You make a compressed, single file of all data, then periodically add a smaller file containing new or deleted data.

Transaction log

You make a copy of a file, then keep in another file details of all changes (transactions) made to the file. If there is a problem, go back to the earlier copy and rerun the changes. Expensive on processing time.

Mirror

This is where a complete system is run in parallel. All changes made to both systems. Costly.

Deliberate corruption

This includes **hackers** and **virus attack**.
Simple security measures include:

- locks on doors and computers
- not leaving printed output lying around

- logging off when leaving a terminal
- using anti-virus software.

Users passwords and levels of access

- People are given **user names and passwords**, which they need to log on to a system.
- Once logged on, they are given a **level of access** by being granted access rights to files and resources by the system administrator.
  - *Access matrix*
    Different users can be given different **access rights** to files. Some might be able to read only, others to write but not delete.
  - *Sub-schemas or 'views'*
    Allow different users to 'see' only certain parts of files, e.g. a doctor's receptionist sees only name and address of patient, while the doctor can see whole record.
- To save time, groups are often given levels of access and then users added to the groups.
- Typical file access rights can be Read only, Execute only, Write, Change, Delete, Create, etc.
- **Resources** can be printers, disk drives etc. to which the user is given access.
- Access can be **time limited** so that the user or group can only log on during certain times.
- **Location can be limited**, so the user or group can only log in on certain machines.
- Often an **audit trail** is also used, e.g. to record when files or resources are accessed. See page 85.

How are passwords cracked?

- Observation (long-range camera).
- Users not changing default passwords e.g. 'password' 'letmein'.
- Using obvious passwords like birthdates or car registrations.
- 'Ghost' log in programs that simulate a log in screen but actually just capture your password.

To stop easy cracking, use **random combination** of letters and numbers, and change it regularly.

Password crackers are programs that try all combinations but take too long if more than six characters.

Encryption

Files can be **encrypted**, so they look like gibberish until **decrypted**. Two common methods are **transposition** and **substitution**.

Transposition: the file is written out in a grid, and instead of reading left to right, it is read top to bottom.

t	h	i	s	.
i	s	.	a	.
c	o	d	e	d
.	l	i	n	e

reads *tic.hsoli.disaen..de*

Figure 13 Encryption

What is this message?
(Hint – numeric vowels)
3og4 u2di 3t hs21u

Substitution: letters are substituted, e.g. numbers for vowels, other letters with next letter in alphabet.

Questions

Core topic 7 Security of data

1. Suggest how and when the following users could protect against accidental corruption of their data:

   a) A medium sized office?
   b) A large branch of an insurance company?
   c) A student?
   d) A small shop?
   e) A branch of a bank or building society?

2. In a network environment, how can users be protected against deliberate corruption of their data?

3. What is an audit trail and how can it be used to help secure data?

4. What is data encryption and how is it used to protect data?

5. What are the common problems associated with passwords?

6. What is a computer virus and how can you protect against it?

Core topic 8

Software capabilities

Often software is compared to benchmarks, i.e. standard results.

Much of the content of this section will be met in hands-on sessions. Often an IT department is required to assess the suitability and capability of software to complete a particular task, so it is necessary to research this information from various sources.

- Software reviews in magazines or on the Internet are an invaluable source of information. Magazines often compare products from different manufacturers, giving you the chance to compare features and prices. Before you buy you must write down a list of requirements; some of these are explained below. Value for money is important, and you should buy enough for your needs and the foreseeable future, but not over-buy.

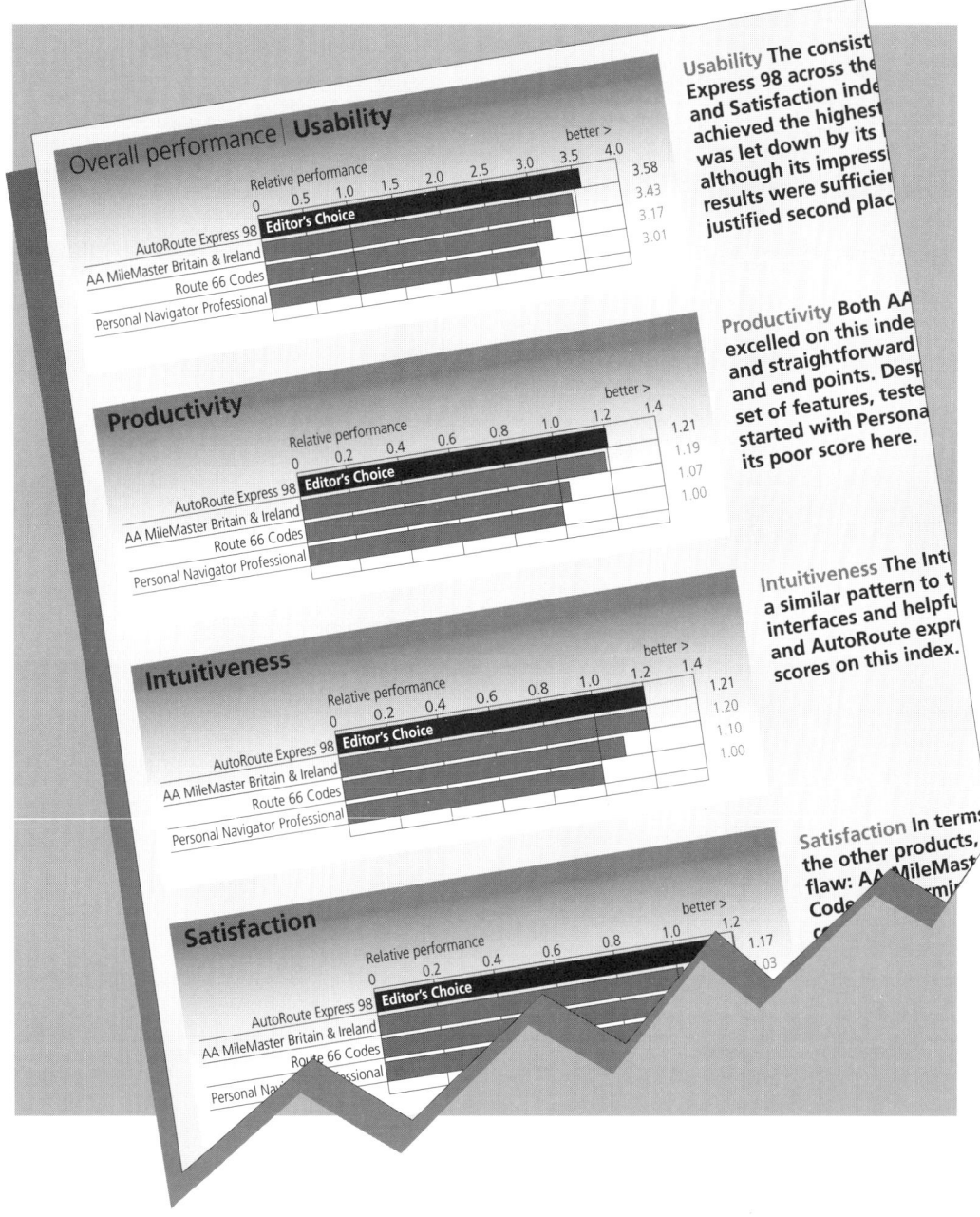

Figure 14 Magazine reviews

- Often companies have standards that restrict choices when buying software, e.g. you can only buy from a given list of software houses, so even if the software is just what you want, you can't buy it.

Some desirable features of packages are explained below:

- *Links to other packages*
  You want to be able to **import or export** your data to other packages – see section on portability of data, page 27. You also want to be able to **embed** (take a snapshot of) or **link** (show latest update of) files from other applications. An embedded spreadsheet in a word-processor will not reflect subsequent changes made to the spreadsheet file, a linked file will.

- *Search facilities*
  You want to be able to find data quickly using **simple or complex searches**. Simple searches would be to enter the required data as the example, more complicated searches would allow the use of wildcard characters so A* would find all data beginning with A, and A??4 would find Asd4 and A984 etc. The ability to use AND conditions to narrow a search and OR to widen it is also useful. Time taken to search (**access times**) should be considered, especially if large data volumes are expected.

- *Macro capabilities.*
  You want to be able to record a sequence of actions and play them back – see page 13.

- *Application generators*
  Modern fourth-generation application packages such as MSAccess are **non-procedural**, allowing you to specify **what** you want to happen not **how** you want it to happen. This means that applications can be rapidly developed and prototyped.

- *Editing*
  With databases it is important to have the ability to change or extend record structures as your needs change.

- *Speed*
  The time taken to perform operations must be acceptable to you.

- *Range of facilities*
  The range of facilities should be sufficient to support the tasks to be undertaken, but not include far too many that will never be utilised.

Extension topic 7

Software to support specialist applications

With the growth of the power of desktop computers, specialist software has also become available at the point where the user requires it.

- This software exists to help manage a range of tasks and applications which might be beyond the scope of generic software such as word-processors, spreadsheets and databases.

Alternatively an application might have a spreadsheet at its heart but have a customised data input or collection screen which prompts users to add their special interest data. Graphs relevant to the interest area can be produced to the exclusion of the general graph types common to spreadsheet packages.

Geographical information systems (GIS)

Geographical information systems providing international statistics on rainfall, deforestation, population changes and hours of sunshine might be an example of this approach.
   Features of such packages might include:

- storage/retrieval of geographical data
- link to global positioning system (GPS)
- output to a range of devices, e.g. screen, printer, plotter, fax and e-mail

- edit/update of data
- design which takes account of expert user
- support for range of input devices including measuring/sampling instruments and satellite surveys
- ability to accept data in a variety of formats, e.g. graphics, whole documents packages
- graphical representation of data
- links to libraries of information via the Internet
- ability to print results – tables, documents, maps (political, economic geological etc.).

Document scanning, storage and retrieval techniques could be used to manipulate regional maps.

Project management

- This software allows project managers to plan and then to plot the progress of a project – for example the installation of a new computer system for a hospital trust or the building of a shopping centre.
- Important decisions regarding the timing of each phase of the operation and the acquisition of specialist equipment in line with the time scale allow costs to be controlled and targets to be met.

Features of such packages might include:

- storage/retrieval of project details
- output to a range of devices, e.g. plotter, printer, Internet transmission
- editing/updating of plans
- complex or multi-featured user interface
- design which takes account of expert engineer/management skills
- support for range of input devices including keyboard, mouse, scanner, digitising tablet
- ability to accept data in a variety of formats, e.g. database fields, spreadsheet calculations
- graphical representation of plans and data.

CAD/CAE/CAM systems (Computer-aided design/Computer-aided engineering/Computer-aided manufacturing or management)

This area of specialist software allows engineers and managers to make the best of their skills and knowledge.

Features of such packages might include:

- storage/retrieval of drawings/designs/data
- simulation facility for engineers/managers
- review facility for different simulations
- output to a range of devices, e.g. screen, printer, plotter, e-mail
- editing/updating of drawings/designs/data
- complex or multi-featured user interface
- design which takes into account expert management/engineer skills
- support for range of input devices, including keyboard, mouse, digitising tablet, scanner
- ability to accept data in a variety of formats, e.g. graphics, output from instruments/monitoring devices and other packages
- auto redraw and resizing
- 3D representation of completed designs
- library of design objects
- print/plot drawings

None of this software will turn an unskilled person into a skilled designer, engineer or manager.

- control of lathes, milling machines and drills (known as computer numeric control – CNC).

A full specification design package such as Autocad will not make a poor design into a good design. It will enable the designer to prepare detailed drawings a lot quicker. It will even enhance the detail and give a three-dimensional view, but it won't make the design more worthy and more functional.

Similarly, computer-aided management will not necessarily improve management decisions if the manager is unable to interpret or use the data delivered by the system.

Mathematical and statistical packages

Like the GISs described above, these packages allow for the rapid interpretation of data and the building of dynamic mathematical models. Many of them are built around spreadsheet 'shells' with the user being directed to exploit specific calculations and presentations for results – most of the formulae and linking text being predetermined by the software designers.

Features of such packages might include:

- storage/retrieval of calculations/formulae/data
- output to a range of devices, e.g. screen, printers, plotters
- editing/updating of data, formulae
- complex or multi-featured user interface
- design which takes account of expert mathematical skills
- support for range of input devices, including keyboard, mouse, instrumentation
- ability to accept data in a variety of formats, e.g. data from other packages
- repetition of calculations and procedures
- graphical representation of data/results
- ability to mix formulae to produce complex models
- simulation of different instruments
- library of graphs, statistical and general computational formulae and procedures
- printing of graphs, results and formulae.

Music composition and editing packages

Now quite commonplace in the music industry, these packages allow musicians to work with and to experiment with different sounds and rhythms.

Features of such packages might include:

- storage/retrieval of compositions
- playback facility
- playback in different modes/keys etc.
- output to a range of devices, e.g. speakers, synthesisers, CD, tape
- editing/updating of compositions
- complex or multi-featured user interface
- design which takes account of expert musician/engineer skills
- support for range of input devices inc. keyboard, mouse, musical instruments, etc.
- ability to accept data in a variety of formats, e.g. live recordings, CD, tape, other packages
- auto-repetition of sounds
- graphical representation of sounds
- ability to mix sounds from several sources
- simulation of different instruments
- library of sound effects
- printing of musical scores.

This kind of package is not a substitute for a talented composer or performer, but a support for their work.

Summary

The above packages are designed:

- to be a reflection of best professional practice
- to improve decision-making
- to enhance professional standards
- to enhance productivity
- to reduce to a minimum time taken by repetitive actions
- to lower or control operational costs
- not to be a substitute for professional skills and judgement.

Provision of software solutions

There are different ways of providing software solutions for specialist applications:

- user-written for specific purpose
- internal development team/ IT department
- external software house to specification
- ready-written standard commercial software.

Reasons for choice

- An external solution does not exist.
- External writers do not understand the problem sufficiently well.
- Skills for writing exist within the company.
- Preparation and development time is available.
- Speed is of the essence.
- Budget will not allow for internal development.
- A tried and trusted solution is available.
- An industry knowledge-base for the problem exists.
- A need to spread the development costs and risks between internal and external departments.
- New software is/is not compatible with existing software base.
- User support overheads incurred by alternative solutions (wide user base/size of supplier organisation and ability to cope with support overheads).
- Compatibility of alternatives with existing hardware base (need for upgrades, additional memory, faster processors, etc.).
- Compatibility with existing software (transferability of existing data files, interface with other generic packages).

The corporate strategy for the selection of software might impose additional restraints upon software purchase. These might conflict with:

- hardware/software purchasing
- licensing agreements.

Questions

Core topic 8 Software capabilities

1 A company wants to purchase some new software. Describe how it can find out what is best for it.

2 Describe the desirable features in a database for:
   a) searching
   b) changing the structure.

3 What is **prototyping** and give reasons for its increase in recent years.

4 When viewing data from other files it is possible to embed or link it. Describe the differences between, and the implications of, each method.

5 When researching for the best word-processor you come across the term 'benchmark'. What is it and why might it be helpful to you?

Extension topic 7 Software to support specialist applications

1 An examination board is considering developing a system which is to be used for maintaining and processing module test results of candidates.

   a) Describe the different ways in which the examination board may be able to provide a software solution.
   b) Discuss the issues the examination board should consider before choosing any particular solution. (NEAB 1997)

Core topic 9: Upgradability

Upgrading is a problem for both the software writers and the software users.
When companies have invested in IT, they have to 'keep up with the Joneses'. This often means upgrading their IT facilities in terms of both hardware and software.

This can be a risky business.

- If you put it off, your **competitors become more productive** and steal market share.
- If you do it too quickly, and the software or hardware is **not proven** and is **unreliable**, again giving competitors the edge.

So it seems you have to strike a careful balance.

Upgrading to newer versions costs money, and the cost benefit has to be weighed in the decision to go ahead.

One of the main problems is researching various options. How do you find out about them if they are at the cutting edge?

A company should use criteria for upgrade, e.g.

- it must be **cost effective**
- there must be a **real need**
- current company **software standards must be maintained**
- **changeover and staff training** must be taken into consideration.

Costs also include retraining of staff.

Case study

SPS is a company that provides a schools' information system. They began circa 1981 using BBC computers, moving to PCs around 1986. They used the standard database package for that time, dBaseIII but didn't move to db4 as it was proving unreliable and the programmers in the company didn't really want to have to rewrite large sections of programs.

However, with the advent of Windows, customers wanted a WIMP interface that had to use existing DOS files, so the company used Clipper, a Windows-based database that used dBaseIII language and files, but it was slower than DOS and the new system hit technical limitations caused by more system requirements and extra modules that the customers demanded.

These included the number of simultaneously open files limit, and large amounts of network traffic.

The company decided to move to client/server technology and now has to support three platforms: DOS, Windows and client/server. The new modules are being phased in, no 'big bang' changeover is possible, so customers have to copy files from old to new system each day to maintain file integrity due to incompatibility of direct use of older files.

So the customers are not happy, and the company is not happy as it has to support lots of different systems.

Nobody made any incorrect decisions, it's just the way it goes!

Questions

Core topic 9 Upgradability

1. Your company uses a package and you are thinking of upgrading to the recently released new version. A competitor has just announced a similar product at a much lower price. What factors would you have to consider before choosing either (or none)?

2. What costs, other than the cost of new software, have to be considered when a software upgrade is proposed?

3. When a software house releases a new version of its software, what support should it give to its customers?

Core topic 10

Reliability of software

To perform the desired tasks software needs to be:

- **reliable,**
- **robust**
- **able to cope with a wide range of user situations.**

- **Software development is expensive** – it takes time to produce reliable software to be sold into a competitive market.
- Whilst under development the software producer is **not earning** revenue from the product.
- There is always **market pressure** to release new software as soon as possible.
- There is **internal company pressure** to start to recover development costs.
- **Reliability** is a balance between these pressures.

Modern large systems are difficult to get error-free. The programs are now so **complex** that every possible combination of inputs cannot be tested in the time available, as the programs have to be brought to market in a reasonable time. It would be no good selling a fully tested and debugged version if it was out of date compared to that of your competitors.

This situation can be eased by:

- using a **modular approach**, where each module is tested before being linked to the others
- using **formal mathematical languages** to develop the systems; if the maths is 'correct', the solution is too.

Testing

The main ways of testing are:

- **functional**, where the system is viewed as a 'black box', and input and output only are examined to see if the system performs as expected. No internal examination of the code is done.

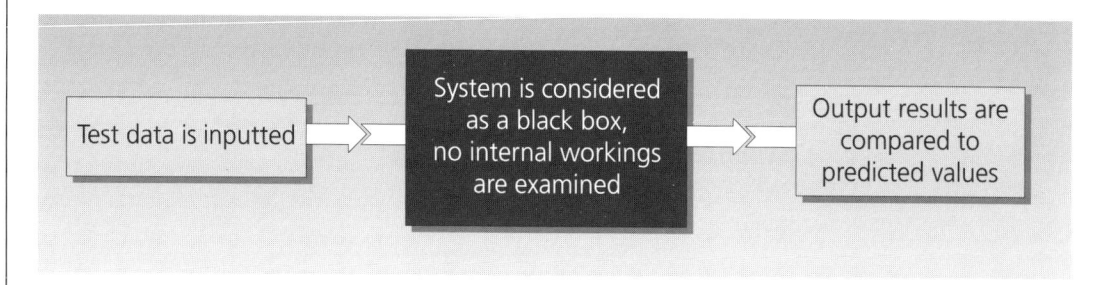

| Test data is inputted | → | System is considered as a black box, no internal workings are examined | → | Output results are compared to predicted values |

Figure 15 Functional testing

- **logical**, where each of the program instructions is tested.
- α, β, γ (**alpha, beta, gamma**), where an internal α copy is tested, then sent out to β site customers, who can use the software free but who have to report any errors in return. After any errors have been corrected the final release version is the γ version. This means the software is tested on machines with many different configurations that a software house could not afford. The number of testing hours is done 'in parallel' by many users rather than at one site.

Space shuttle

It costs a great deal to test software thoroughly. The most expensive piece of code is supposed to be the control program for the space shuttle. Just what can happen if testing is not done properly can be seen in what happened to the Ariane space rocket, when European experts confirmed that the loss of the prototype Ariane 5 rocket – the climax of a £5,000,000,000 attempt to capture a larger share of the space launch business – could be blamed on specification and design errors in the software of the rocket's guidance system.

Questions

Core topic 10 Reliability of software

1. Software can never be 100% reliable – discuss.

2. What are formal methods in relation to software reliability?

3. Why might a software house release a program with errors?

4. What is the difference between functional and logical testing?

5. Some programs are tested much more thoroughly than others. Suggest reasons for this and give examples.

6. Why does most software have bugs?

Core topic 11: Configurability of hard/software

This is about the setting up and matching of hardware to software to get the best out of them. It is no good having really powerful hardware matched to incorrectly set up software and vice versa.

Hardware set-up

Overall performance is only as strong as the weakest link.

A few years ago, if you wanted to install a new hard drive, this involved a great deal of **time and effort**.

- The manuals for the computer, the existing hard drive controller card and the new drive had to be read.
- 'Jumpers' (links connecting small pins on the circuit board) had to be altered on the disk drive to select master/slave settings and jumpers on the card also needed to be changed.

Even buying a new printer was fraught with problems.

- You had to consider the interface type, e.g. serial or parallel.
- Then switches called dip switches *inside* the printer had to be altered to select the character set (IBM, ASCII, Epson).
- Then the software had to be installed to drive the printer from each application, so a driver disk had to be used to install drivers for Windows and DOS programs. (Without these, the printer's capabilities could not be used.)

> A school bought a colour printer for the Archimedes. When they moved to PCs there were no drivers for it, so they had no colour printouts. They used the nearest driver when it became available, but it still printed incorrect colours.

Drivers can be quite easily downloaded from the Internet.

- The **incorrect** version of a driver can lead to **unexpected results**, either a lack of features or no results at all.

Plug and play or Plug and pray?

Nowadays the process is a little less painless with '**plug and play**' systems.

- The configuration of the hardware is no longer controlled by jumpers and dip switches but by electrically alterable read-only memory (EAROM).
- This configured with set-up software programs, or even directly by the operating system that detects its presence.
- When recently fitting a new disk drive on a network server, although we still had to set a jumper on the drive, after switch on, the operating system detected the new hardware and led us through the process of setting it up.

Hardware driver programs

Peripherals (hardware) added to your machine require driver programs to look after them.

Driver on your machine	What it controls
screen	- resolution - colours - must have matching video card (no good installing a 16 million colour driver if your video card or monitor doesn't support it)
keyboard	- language - key actions - number of keys - type of keyboard
mouse	- resolution of movement - which button does what - type of interface (serial etc.)
printer	- fonts and bitmaps - resolution (dots per inch)
net	- type of medium, co-axial twisted pair - protocol, etc.

Questions

Core topic 11 Configurability of hard/software

1 What is a driver program and why is it necessary?

2 What might be the effects of installing an incorrect printer driver?

3 How has the process of configuring hardware changed over recent years?

4 You have a powerful computer but it is performing poorly and you suspect someone has changed some settings. A friend suggests that you check your drivers and run your hardware set-up software. What does this mean and how might it help you?

5 Why were 'plug and play' systems developed?

6 What are jumpers and dip switches and what are the more modern equivalent?

Core topic 12: Modes of processing

How quickly the output from a system is required is a major factor in determining the mode of processing.

Batch processing

- When the data can be **gathered over a period of time** then processed at once
- and/or the output is not required immediately.
- A typical example is payroll. This has both features; the output is not required immediately and the data is gathered and processed once a month.
- The data can be prepared off-line to the main computer, using key to disk methods.
- Another good example is mail-order.

Interactive processing

- This means you are interacting with a computer **but it does not necessarily mean that the processing is done immediately**.
- With some systems you interact with the computer, and your transaction is recorded, but only carried out later in a batch update run. For example, some stores with their own debit cards use this system as it is more cost-effective to connect to head office once a day than to have an expensive line open all day.

Transaction processing (pseudo real-time)

- The processing is done as **quickly as possible**, where not to do so can cause problems.
- In a airline seat reservation system, if this is not done you could end up with double bookings.
- It involves locking records so other users can't overwrite them.
- If the booking is declined, the record is released.
- If not, the record is updated as taken.

Real-time

- In control situations where the computer is e.g. guiding a rocket, the processing has to keep up with real time, **it can't lag behind**.
- It would be no use an autopilot coming up with the command 'raise flaps' two seconds after you hit the ground!
- The output is available quickly enough to affect the input.

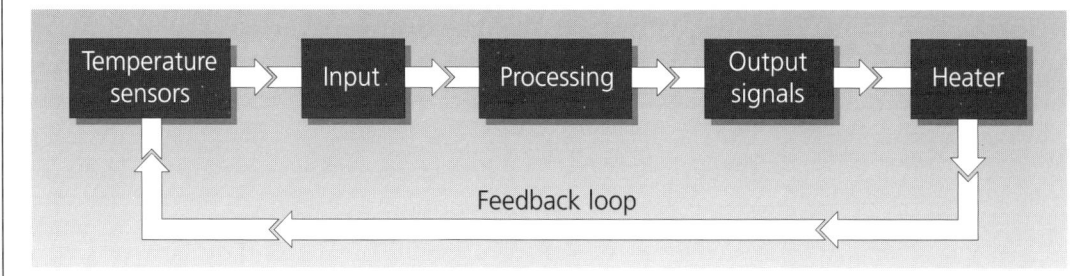

Figure 16 Real-time processing with feedback

Data types and how they are processed

Text

- Text is held as strings of characters, each character occupies a byte (8 bits) of memory.
- Strings can be joined, split, searched, etc.

Pictures

There are two types of images:
- pixel-based (or bitmaps)
- vector-based.

For pixel-based pictures see section on scanners (page 8).

Vector images are used on CAD/CAM systems (Computer-aided design/manufacture) e.g. to save a file consisting of a circle, instead of a map of each pixel, the centre co-ordinates and the radius are stored. So **co-ordinates and measurements** are used to describe shapes.

Numbers

Numbers can be stored in a fixed number of bytes

- as integers
- as real numbers
- or sometimes when accuracy is needed, in a variable number of bytes: as the binary equivalent of decimals (Binary Coded Decimal – BCD).

Integers are
- accurate and fast for calculation
- limited in range.

Real numbers
- have a bigger range
- but are less accurate and slower as they use a 'standard form' approach
- take typically two or four bytes respectively per number.

BCD
- is more like storing the number as a string
- can take lots of storage, depending on the length of the number
- each digit takes a nybble (half a byte!)
- BCD is accurate but slow.

Sound

Sound patterns can be sampled and stored and/or processed for later playback.

- This takes a lot of memory e.g. 3-minute stereo song where the waveform is sampled at CD quality (44,000 times a second) takes about 40 Mbyte of space.
- The file is made up of the **readings** taken.
- Each reading is made up of a 16 bit binary number (two bytes of information).
- If fewer samples are taken, or fewer bits used for each sample, the **quality goes down**.
- If fewer readings (samples) are taken per second then there are more 'gaps' where you don't know what the signal was doing.
- If fewer bits are used, then the readings take a smaller range of values.
- Eight bits give only 256 possible values whereas 16 bits gives 65,000, therefore a much finer resolution between readings can be made.

- For example, if maximum value is 10 volts and minimum is 0, with eight bits the resolution is 10/256 =.039v, with 16 bits the resolution is approx. 10/65,000 = 0.00015 volt

Questions

Core topic 12 Modes of processing

1. What features of an IT task would you consider when choosing a mode of operation?

2. How does the type of data influence the type of processing that can be performed on the data? Give examples.

3. Explain with examples what is meant by real-time processing.

4. What features of an IT task would lend it to batch processing?

5. Explain the term on-line processing.

6. Why is it necessary to use pseudo real-time processing in some situations?

7. What mode of processing would you use for the following situations? Give reasons.

   a) Processing mail-order requests.
   b) Controlling a submarine.
   c) Selling airline seats by telephone.

8. Explain how the quality of sound sampling is affected by sampling rate and bits per sample.

9. Giving reasons, what type of number storage would you use for:

   a) whole numbers?
   b) the distances between planets?
   c) recording a land speed record attempt?
   d) currency conversion?

10. Why is a pixel-based file of a coloured circle larger than a vector-based file of the same image?

Core topic 13

Relational databases

- Traditional flat-file systems are **program oriented,** i.e. a program is written that says what data is to be stored and how it is to be stored.
- If other fields of information need to be added at a later date, then all the programs have to be altered.
- Database management systems (DBMS) are **data oriented**, you only have to say **what** you want to store, not **how**.
- This gives you **program–data independence**.
- With the flat-file approach, lots of data is duplicated (i.e. redundant), and these multiple copies lead to mistakes e.g. in typing in, or updating just some of them.
- This results in poor **data integrity** (correctness).
- DBMS can enforce referential integrity e.g. you can't loan a video with ID 001 in the loans table, if video with ID 001 doesn't exist in the video table.
- DBMS also have better security (see page 91).
- With a centralised approach, rather than a collection of dispersed files for different purposes, a single set of data can be used, with different views of the same data for the different applications.

For example with flat files, names and addresses might be kept in both Payroll and Personnel files. With DBMS they are kept only once, with both applications seeing the same data and any other fields relevant to their application.

The co-ordination of who's allowed to see what, what is kept in the database, users etc. is done by a database administrator.

- S/he has responsibility for the database, its **structure**, **contents** and **security** (against both accidental and deliberate corruption).
- S/he must also **monitor the performance** of the database and reorganise it if necessary.
- Requests for alteration to structure, new reports, etc. are channelled through the administrator so that there are not 'too many cooks'.

> ### Example: Flat file video rental shop
> If all information about loans had to be kept in a single file there would be lots of duplication of data.
> You would also need two other files (not linked), for video details and customer details.
> This gives the user problems, e.g. trying to calculate overdues.

Database solution

The most popular database is the relational database, the structure of which is determined by the process of **normalisation** of the data.

Normalisation is the process of organising data into tables to minimise data duplication.

The formal way of doing it is described on the following pages in four steps.

> Note that File/Record/Field, Table/Row/Column and Entity/Tuple/Attribute mean the same, and shouldn't be interchanged (but often are!).

Step 1

a) List all the data items to be stored in the database (sometimes called the **schema**).

Cust_id, Surname, Forename, Date_of_birth, Postcode, Isbn, Title, Vid, Cost_to_buy, Cost_to_rent, Supplier, Date_out, Date_in

b) Identify an **entity** and a single (atomic) **key** – underline it.

CUSTOMER (<u>Cust id</u>, Surname, Forename, Date_of_birth, Postcode, Isbn, Title, Vid, Cost_to_buy, Cost_to_rent, Supplier, Date_out, Date_in)

c) For a **single instance** of the key, which fields would form a list (repeating group)?

Cust_id	Surname	Forename	Date_of_birth	Postcode	Isbn	Title	Vid	Cost_to_buy	Cost_to_rent	Supplier	Date_in	Date_out
001,	Smith	Fred	01/01/72	WA3 7QD	1-85805-170-4	Star Wars	032	100	2	whsmith	01/01/97	03/01/97
					1-85506-120-3	Empire	034	100	2	whsmith	04/01/97	06/03/97
					1-865678-134-4	Jedi	037	100	2	whsmith	07/03/97	11/03/97

d) Identify the repeating group, using brackets or italics.

CUSTOMER (<u>Cust id</u>, Surname, Forename, Date_of_birth, Postcode, [Isbn, Title, Vid, Cost_to_buy, Cost_to_rent, Supplier, Date_out, Date_in])

This is the un-normalised form (UNF).

Step 2

a) Remove the **repeating group**, along with a **copy of the key**, to a **new table**.

CUSTOMER (<u>Cust id</u>, Surname, Forename, Date_of_birth, Postcode)
NEW TABLE (Cust_id, Isbn, Title, Vid, Cost_to_buy, Cost_to_rent, Supplier, Date_out, Date_in)

b) Identify an **entity** and a **key**.

LOAN (<u>Cust id</u>, Isbn, Title, Vid, Cost_to_buy, Cost_to_rent, Supplier, Date_out, Date_in)

What should be the key?

This is the most difficult bit, and you have to think really hard to see what the effect of a **key combination** means in practice:

> This is the hardest bit.

Cust_id	Isbn	Title	Vid	Cost_to_buy	Cost_to_rent	Supplier	Date_out	Date_in
001	1-80765-234-5	never say never	007	67.00	2.00	w h smith	1/2/98	

a) try Cust_id

but this means **only one row is allowed per Cust_id** therefore only one loan ever possible for each customer. As soon as you try to input another record for customer 001, an error will occur.

b) try Vid,

only one row allowed per Vid, so each video **can only be rented once**, ever!

c) try Cust_id +Vid

only one row allowed per Cust_id/Vid combination, so you can only rent that video once to that customer, ever. **They can't rent it again two months later.**

d) better to have Cust_id+Vid+date_out, so a customer can re-rent at a later date as well.

We now have **first normal form (1NF)**.

CUSTOMER (<u>Cust id</u>, Surname, Forename, Date_of_birth, Postcode)
LOAN (<u>Cust id</u>, Isbn, Title, <u>Vid</u>, Cost_To_Buy, Cost_To_Rent, Supplier, <u>Date out</u>, Date_in)

Step 3

Atomic tables are always in second normal form so we only have to consider tables with **compound keys**.

We have to ask the question:

Do all non-key fields depend on the whole of the key or only part of the key?

(You might find it easier to ask it in a slightly different manner: Is this non-key field a property of the whole of the key or only part of the key?)

LOAN (<u>Cust id</u>, Isbn, Title, <u>Vid</u>, Cost_to_buy, Cost_to_rent, Supplier, <u>Date out</u>, Date_in)

Looking at the **non-key** fields:

Isbn and Title are **properties** of the video, not of who takes it or when, so is Cost_to_buy and Cost_to_rent. (We assume there is a flat cost_to_rent charge for the life of the video, irrespective of who it is to be loaned to i.e. no junior loans.) Supplier depends on the video also.

The Date_in depends on the loan (you couldn't put Date_in in the customer table, for example, as this would mean the customer could only return videos on one date!).

So remove the **partial dependent** fields to a new table with a **copy of the part of the key** they depend on.

CUSTOMER (<u>Cust id</u>, Surname, Forename, Date_of_birth, Postcode)
LOAN (<u>Cust id</u>, <u>Vid</u>, <u>Date out</u>, Date_in)
VIDEO (<u>Vid</u>, Isbn, Title, Cost_to_buy, Cost_to_rent, Supplier)

We now have **second normal form (2NF)**.

Note Vid is key not Isbn as we usually have more than one copy of a video that all have the same Isbn, whereas the Vid is unique.

Step 4

All **non-key fields** must depend only on the key and nothing else. There must be **no chance of confusion**.

CUSTOMER (<u>Cust id</u>, Surname, Forename, Date_of_birth, Postcode)
LOAN (<u>Cust id</u>, <u>Vid</u>, <u>Date out</u>, Date_in)
VIDEO (<u>Vid</u>, Isbn, Title, Cost_to_buy, Cost_to_rent, Supplier)

For two copies of a video, the title is the same and depends on the Isbn not the Vid, so do the other fields. So add another table for COPIES OF VIDEOS, leaving Isbn as **foreign key**.

The only other problem is supplier, e.g. WHSMITH, has **more than one branch**, so if you bought from more than one branch you'd have to identify which, so add an extra table to give **third normal form (3NF)**.

CUSTOMER (<u>Cust id</u>, Surname, Forename, Date_of_birth, Postcode)
LOAN (<u>Cust Id</u>, <u>Vid</u>, <u>Date out</u>, Date_in)
VIDEO (<u>Vid</u>, Title, Cost_to_buy, Cost_to_rent, Sid)
COPIESOFVIDEO (<u>Vid</u>, <u>Isbn</u>)
SUPPLIER (<u>Sid</u>, name, address)

Whew! The alternative is to identify the entities CUSTOMER, VIDEO, LOAN, SUPPLIER and allocate fields to each from the initial data to be stored (by asking which entity does this depend on), then work out the keys. With practice this can be quicker but is more hit and miss.

With either approach, an **entity relationship (E/R) diagram** can be drawn to show the relationships between the tables.

RELATIONAL DATABASES 49

Using E/R diagrams to find entities

As a first stab there appear to be two entities – **Customer** and **Vid**.

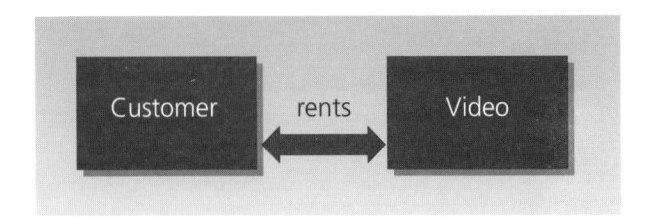

Figure 17

Note that to find the **order** of a relationship (1 : 1, 1 : Many, Many to many), you should look at **both ends** of the relationship. For example, one VIDEO has many COPIESOFVIDEO, and one COPIESOFVIDEO is of one VIDEO, therefore the relationship is 1 : many.

Now, one customer rents many COPIESOFVIDEOS, and from the other side, one COPYOFVIDEO is loaned to many customers, so it's many : many.

In a relational database, **many : many** relationships are not allowed and a **linking table** has to be created. In this case, it's LOAN. So:
- one CUSTOMER has many LOANS, and a LOAN is to one CUSTOMER => 1: many
- one COPIESOFVIDEO has many LOANS and one LOAN concerns one COPYOFVIDEO => 1: many

- we could add the entity supplier as: one supplier supplies many videos => 1: many

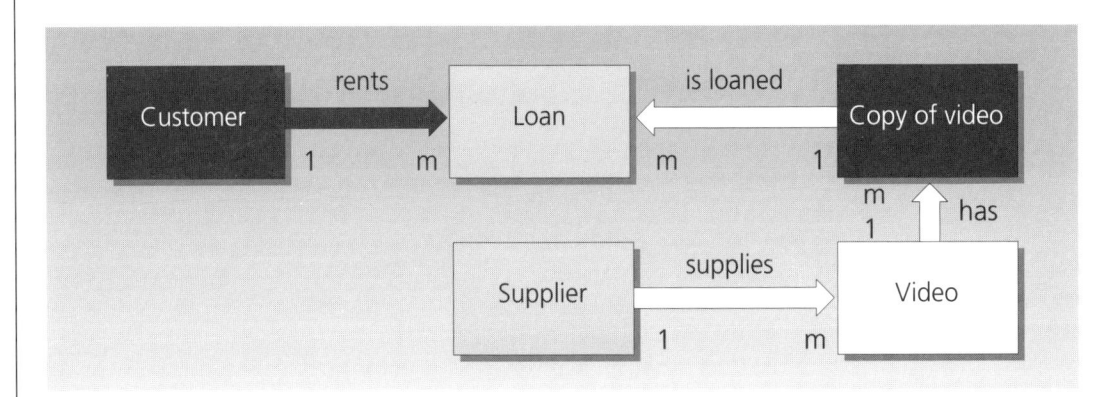

Figure 18 Entity/relationship diagram

Data types

The next step in database design is to choose the data types for each field. Common types are:

- text (gives maximum length),
- number (integer or real),
- logical, sometimes called Boolean (true or false),
- date
- currency etc.

Note that some field types, e.g. date, have auto-validation properties, i.e. just by giving it that type, you can't enter 32/1/97. At this stage validation checks such as range checks, etc. should be decided on.

If you want to see the data in a particular order, then an index should be created for the field to allow this to happen quickly. An index keeps a list of the natural record numbers for that sequence. So if the natural order to the data is:

1 Smith John 1/1/67
2 Jones Susan 2/3/76
3 Bloggs Fred 1/1/52

then an alphabetical index (ascending) would be 3,2,1, whilst a date of birth index would be 3,1,2.

Questions

Core topic 13 Relational databases

1 What does the term **program-data independence** mean?

2 In a flat-file system there is said to be data duplication. Explain this term with the aid of an example.

3 Compare and contrast **program oriented** and **data oriented** file systems.

4 What is a database administrator and what do they do?

5 An orders table in a database is defined as:

   Order (OrderNumber, date, StockNumber, quantity)

   What problems can you see if this is implemented and how can they be overcome?

6 Describe with the aid of diagrams how an entity relationship diagram can be developed.

7 Develop an entity relationship diagram for Book and Author, showing your reasoning.

8 What is the partial dependency test performed during data normalisation?

9 How is security implemented on a DBMS?

10 What is referential integrity and how can a database enforce it?

11 What is the process of data normalisation for?

RELATIONAL DATABASES 51

Core topic 14: Verification/validation

There are many ways in which errors can occur in IT systems. This section describes some of them and the measures taken to reduce them.

During manual data capture, data can be **transcribed** from the human to machine readable form incorrectly e.g. numbers can be **transposed**, so 1235 is keyed as 1253. To avoid this, two methods can be used.

- The first is when the data is keyed in twice by different operators. The two versions are compared and if they are the same they are accepted, if different, rejected. This process is known as **verification**.

- The other method is an example data **validation** (a check to see if the data is **sensible**), where the computer program has rules about which data to accept and reject. The one that can spot transposition errors is the Check Digit Check, usually used for long account numbers etc.

Verify, type twice.

Valid = sensible.

Data validation checks

Check digit

An extra digit is added to the end of all account numbers, using a special calculation. When a number is keyed in, the computer can

- take off the last digit
- do the calculation on the others and see if the check digit it calculates agrees with the one typed in.

If not, there has been a typing error.
Some methods use two digits or more, and can actually correct the error!

Example: The modulus 11 method (a common form of check digit)
To add new check digit:

- write down number, add a weighting factor underneath, starting from right-hand side

    1 2 3 2   original number
    5 4 3 2   weighting
    5 8 9 4   product of weighting times digit

- add this up = 5+8+9+4=26
- divide by 11 and note the remainder = 2 remainder 4
- now take the remainder number from 11, to get the check digit (if it is 10 use **x** as the digit); so taking 4 from 11 gives a check digit **7**.

New account number is 12327.

Suppose this is keyed in as 12237, the computer does the same sum:

1 2 2 3   number
5 4 3 2   weighting
5 8 **6 6**   product

so this adds up to 25, dividing by 11 gives 2 remainder 3. This is subtracted from 11 to give as 8<>7 therefore an incorrect code has been found.

Range check (between)

Data must lie within a range e.g. for height in metres the rule might be: >1.00 and <=2.00

Data that lies at the end of ranges is called extreme data. Would the following be rejected or accepted?

    1.00   2.00   1.211   0.99

Presence check (required)

A field **has** to be filled in. So surname would be required, a phone number would not be as not everyone has a phone.

Lookup (like)

The data keyed in must **match a list**, e.g. LIKE 'RED' or 'GREEN' or 'AMBER'

Picture check (mask)

The data keyed in must **match a pattern** of letters and numbers, e.g. a post code might be LL9?9LL where L is letter, 9 is digit and ? is number or space.

Length check (character count)

The number of characters **does not exceed a limit**, e.g. surname (30).

Built-in data type checks (auto-validation)

If data field is defined as a DATE type, then it will **automatically rejec**t incorrect date inputs such as 31/13/97.

Data transmission checks

When data is transmitted from one place to another, it takes the form of binary numbers, a series of 0s and 1s, usually sent in groups of eight called bytes. There is a chance of the binary codes being corrupted, so error checking data must also be sent, to be checked when the data is received. There are two main ways of doing this.

Parity check

In this check,
- an **extra bit** is sent along with each group (normally one group contains one character), as it is transmitted.
- This parity bit is set to 0 or 1 to '**pair off**' the number of 1s in the group.
- When the group is received, the number of 1s are checked and if the 1s don't pair off, the group has to be retransmitted.
- This method **cannot find double errors**.

Checksum

- Bytes are normally sent in blocks of 256.
- Each byte transmitted is added to the checksum byte and any overflow ignored (a bit like 9+8+3+5+6+3=(3)4).

VERIFICATION/VALIDATION 53

- The **checksum byte** is sent at the **end of the block**.
- On reception, the bytes received are **added up in a similar fashion** and the final block total should match the checksum byte.
- If not, the **whole block of bytes has to be retransmitted**.
- This method **can handle double errors**.

Questions

Core topic 14 Verification/validation

1 Describe the difference between data validation and data verification.

2 Explain the term data integrity.

3 Describe three validation checks you have used.

4 When data is transmitted validation checks are often performed. What is the purpose of the checks and describe one in detail?

5 What is a transposition error and how can it be avoided?

6 Why are check digits used and how do they work?

7 What is a transcription error and what steps can be taken to minimise them?

Core topic 15: Data, information and knowledge

Data is processed to yield information.

Data is raw values relating to facts, events or transactions, e.g. data recorded when buying a tin of beans.

Information is processed data, e.g. the data concerning sales is processed to produce statistical information such as total value of today's sales.

Knowledge is the use of information in context, e.g. if I know today's sales of beans and sales trends I can predict how many will be sold tomorrow.

Data can also be captured by a number of means:

- directly, e.g. MICR, OMR (see page 9)
- or input via other means, e.g. key-to-disk: data preparation of the amounts on cheques.

Note: MICR only reads the account number and sort code, the actual value of the cheque has to be keyed in by hand.

Any system that **transcribes** data (re-keys it) is open to human error.

- Letters and numbers can be **transposed**.
- Verification and validation checks must be used to ensure accuracy (see page 52).

In a data processing system the flow of data into and out of the system must be controlled.

- A **Data Control system** will be in place.
- This will record the arrival, entering, acceptance and release of data in the system so that its **progress can be monitored** and no data can get lost in the system.

Information has many characteristics and can be classified in many ways:

1 Level

Operational
- Data processing operations at a **day-to-day level** produce data, e.g. a supermarket selling baked beans.
- The data captured will be date, time, till, worker, product, quantity, along with payment details.

Tactical
- The data captured above can be **processed to yield management information**, e.g. total bean sales, profit etc., and can be used to make tactical decisions, e.g. move product on shelf, reduce price etc.

Strategic
- Models and expert systems can be fed the data to produce **what if** predictions, upon which **strategic decisions** can be made. This level is for the senior management and is often called **decision support**.

An **expert system** consists of:

- a **knowledge base** of facts and rules
- an **inference engine** which is a program that allows interrogation of the knowledge base
- and a **user interface** to allow the user to ask the questions in a non-mathematical way.

A typical example could be a knowledge base of flight times and destinations from a number of airports as the facts; the rules would concern whether a connecting flight could be made.

- The question might be 'Can I get a flight from UK to JFK airport today?'
- The inference engine would search the facts, using the rules, to suggest answers.
- An important advantage of the expert system approach is that it can easily take into account cancellations etc. by simple alteration of the facts.
- No reprogramming is required.

Expert systems are set up by **information engineers**, who specialise in gathering the facts and rules of a current human system and creating an expert system.

- The final system might be the sum total of a number of specialists' life-long learning.
- Their introduction into businesses can threaten the resident experts.

2 Source

Internal, external, primary, secondary.

3 Nature

Data can be **quantitative**, i.e. measured (e.g. height) or **qualitative** i.e. a judgement about something, e.g. tall, (formal, informal).

4 Time

Data can concern **historical** events, **current** events or **future** predictions.

5 Frequency

This concerns **how often** data is captured. Data can be gathered in real time, e.g. controlling a power station, hourly, e.g. temperature readings or other data logging, or daily/monthly e.g. time sheets.

6 Form

The form the data takes can be **written**, **visual**, e.g. pictures and graphs, **aural**, e.g. speech, **sensory**, i.e. taken from sensors, e.g. temperature.

7 Type

The type of data can be **detailed**, e.g. every reading, **aggregated**, e.g. the sum of the readings over a period, **sampled** readings only taken at certain intervals.

Quality of data

- A common IT term is GIGO – garbage in, garbage out.
- Mistakes can occur in data capture resulting in the £1,000,000 gas bill.
- The **coarseness** of data can prove a problem when it is processed, e.g. heights are recorded correct to nearest 10 cm, then the average height calculated to 2 decimal places.
- **Data can age.** It is important for data to be date stamped as the integrity (correctness) of data declines with age. Also there is a danger of overwriting newer data with older versions if this is not done.

Are school timetables same as September version?

Suppose a database holds a photograph of an individual who changes hair colour etc.

How much of Guinness Book of Records 1956 is still valid?

56 INFORMATION TECHNOLOGY REVISION NOTES

- Ambiguous systems for coding can also coarsen data. For example, red blue green may be coded RBG for speed. What about bluey greens? There is also a problem if the coding system is lost, e.g. RBG=red black green?
- **Subjective data** can also give concern. For example, if results are coded 'good', 'poor', 'bad', you might grade as poor, someone else grades the same work as bad.

'Good' information is:

- relevant to the task
- accurate
- correct (data can be accurate to 2 decimal places but incorrect – see above average height example)
- complete
- delivered to the right person
- at the right time
- in the right amount of detail
- via the correct channel of communication
- in an understandable form.

Bad information is irrelevant, inaccurate, incorrect, incomplete, or delivered to the wrong person at the wrong time in the wrong amount of detail, or by the back door and is incomprehensible!

Extension topic 8

Note this definition – data which has meaning!

Information

The definition of information, as far as management systems are concerned, is **data which has meaning** to the person receiving it or data which has been processed into a meaningful format.

- The preparation of information requires knowledge about the person or groups who are to receive it.
- This is known as the 'context' for the information – the circumstances in which it is to be used.
- The information needs to be helpful and supportive of the business activity. Information has no value in itself, unless it is able to influence the decision-making process of the business.

Information has many characteristics, in addition to the general points made above.

The following tables summarise some examples:

Source	Nature	Level
internal	quantitative	strategic
external	qualitative	tactical
primary	formal	operational
secondary	informal	

Time	Frequency	Use	Form	Type
historical	real time	planning	written	detailed
current	hourly	control	visual	aggregated
future	daily	decision	aural	sampled
	monthly		sensory	

Without an efficient way of sorting and organising, data managers could end up with a great deal of data but very little information.

It is often assumed that the more speedy the management information system is, and the more up-to-date the information, then the better the decision-making will become. This may be true, but bear in mind that decisions are taken by managers and they can get it wrong!

> The RMS Titanic (1912) was not lost due to a lack of information about the presence of icebergs but misjudgement about how to navigate the ship in the conditions!

There is no universally acceptable way of presenting information.

- Businesses develop their own standards, some of which are supported by professional bodies, and in some cases because of commercial law.

The differences may arise because:

- a business may require information and data to be handled in a certain manner, maybe for the sake of speed and convenience
- familiarity with a business's operations and description of its products might lead to a kind of 'shorthand' which is only meaningful to employees
- customers and local or national government departments might want the information delivered in a different format.

Examples

- Customers might require a full description of their purchase and would not be satisfied with a coded reference.
- National government requires tax returns to be presented on the appropriate forms showing the correct detail.
- Company reports, such as might appear in the press or be presented at shareholders' meetings, are not likely to show information which could be helpful to a business rival.

There are no hard and fast definitions of what characterises good information, other than **'good information is what you find useful'**. The definition of 'good' changes for a given context.

For example:

- at an **operational level** information has to be precise. If a customer orders materials to a given standard, quantity and price then the invoice should show these items. It is unhelpful to show approximations.
- At a **tactical level**, however, production figures to the nearest hundred or thousand might be all that is required to make some marketing judgement.
- Whilst at a **strategic level**, roundings of a higher order would be sufficient for long-term planning, where there is even less certainty.

Extension topic 9

Data

In everyday speech 'data' and 'information' tend to have the same meaning. However, from the point of view of a management information system (MIS) the meanings are distinct.

Common exam question: Distinguish between data and information.

- **Data are events**, occurrences, observations, recorded facts, transactions and the like. They form the raw material from which information is produced.
- **Information is the processed form** of data which has meaning for those for whom it is intended.

Data are facts obtained by reading, observation, measuring, weighing and recording. They are the product of some sort of activity – natural or man-made.

For example:

- Volcanic disturbance can give rise to shock waves, temperature and pressure changes, emission of toxic gases, all of which can be recorded, as raw data, and then processed in some way to help geologists understand more about volcanoes.

- Business gives rise to production of goods, sales figures, invoices, bank accounts, advertising costs, wages, exports. Again all these can be recorded and processed in order to give economists an idea of how we use resources.

- Data can arise either as a '**by-product**' of some operation or as part of a specially created recording system.
    - For example the volcanic action, referred to above, gives rise to things which are recordable, but an invoice has to be created from several business activities and a system setup to produce it.

- Data may **require translation** or transcription prior to entry into the system. This can affect the accuracy of the data:
    - it could be miskeyed by the data processing operative
    - it could be misinterpreted, especially if the data is in a foreign language
    - it could be misinterpreted because the data processing operator didn't understand the units in which the data was presented.

The quantity and quality of data capture can lead to inaccuracy and misjudgements.

The amount of data generated from within a business or organisation is tremendous. Some of it is useful; some of it is not. However, the sheer bulk means that managers have to be selective about what they use.

The quality (reliability) of some of the data could be suspect.

For example:

- A builders' merchant allowed customers to measure out quantities of sand and gravel by the 'shovel full'. The numbers were used to invoice the customer and to calculate profits.

- County council employees on a traffic survey filled in the census returns without counting the vehicles. The data was going to be used to plan a road-widening scheme in a congested area.

Questions

Core topic 15 Data, information and knowledge

1 Define the terms **data**, **information** and **knowledge**.

2 What is **coarseness of data** and how can it affect the quality of information?

3 Why is it important for data to be date-stamped?

4 How can the encoding of information produce problems?

5 Name and describe four typical classifications of information.

6 Give four characteristics of 'bad' information.

Questions

Extension topic 8 Information

1 A school is planning the introduction of a computer-based attendance system for classes and registration groups. The purpose of the system is to produce information for the following end-users:

- class teachers
- pastoral managers (tutors/heads of year)
- senior managers (e.g. Deputy Head).

For each of the different end-users describe, with the aid of an example, information that the system might produce in relation to their requirements. (NEAB 1997)

Core topic 16 — Effective presentation

When information is presented to an audience, the method and style of presentation is important. The following factors might be considered:

- The **age of the audience** (including the reading age) will be a factor if the message is textual.
- Sometimes a **picture or graphic** can explain an idea more effectively.

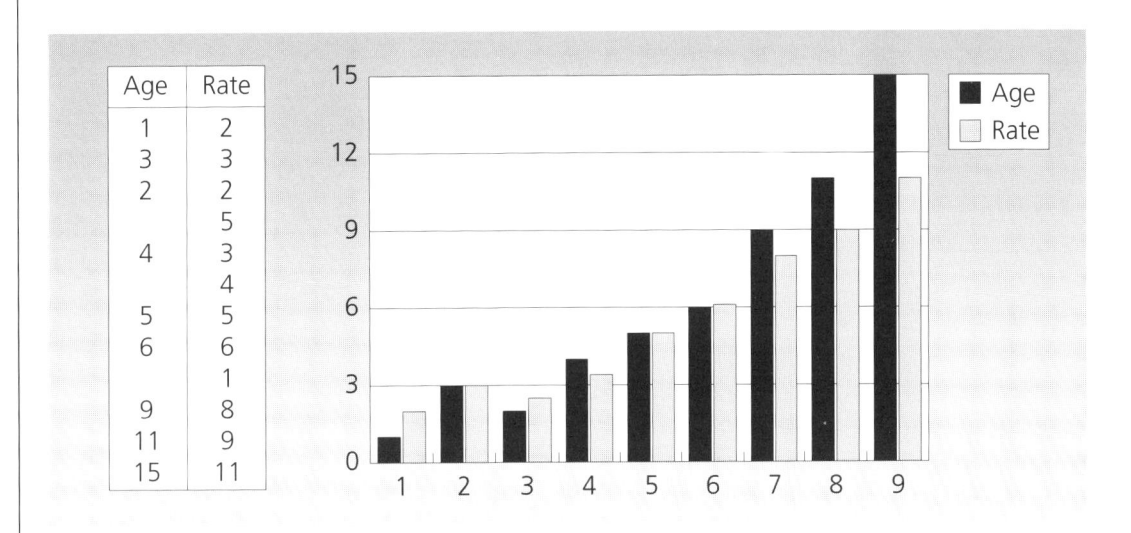

Age	Rate
1	2
3	3
2	2
	5
4	3
	4
5	5
6	6
	1
9	8
11	9
15	11

Figure 19 Words vs pictures

Try to use diagrams in any exam question when explanations are called for.

- The **language** used should be appropriate; you would not use technical terms to a non-technical audience.
- The **length of the message** is important. Don't get bogged down in too much detail and lose the interest of the audience.
- The use of **humour** in some contexts can enliven proceedings and make events more memorable.

Questions

Core topic 16 Effective presentation

1. How might an IT presentation made to an infant school differ from one made to a company annual general meeting?

2. How can a presentation be made more effective?

3. After a presentation a customer remarked that the presenter had not used appropriate language. What was meant by this?

Extension topic 10

Organisational structure

Organisational structures determine the flow of information.

Understanding the basic concepts of organisational structure

The internal structure will take into account such things as:

- **the relationships between individuals**
- **who is in charge**
- **who has authority to make decisions**
- **who carries out decisions**
- **how information is communicated.**

This is often known as **the formal organisation of the business**. Although organisations will vary from one business to another, there are some similarities.

- For example, many large companies are controlled by a few directors, are divided into departments with managers and section heads and have many workers in each department.

One method of organising a business is to put people together to work effectively, based on their skills and abilities. The structure is built up or develops as a result of the employees of the business.

In contrast a structure could be created first, with all appropriate job positions outlined, and then people employed to fill them.

Many companies use organisation charts to show the structure.

- These also help to show communication problems and allow individuals to see their position in the company.

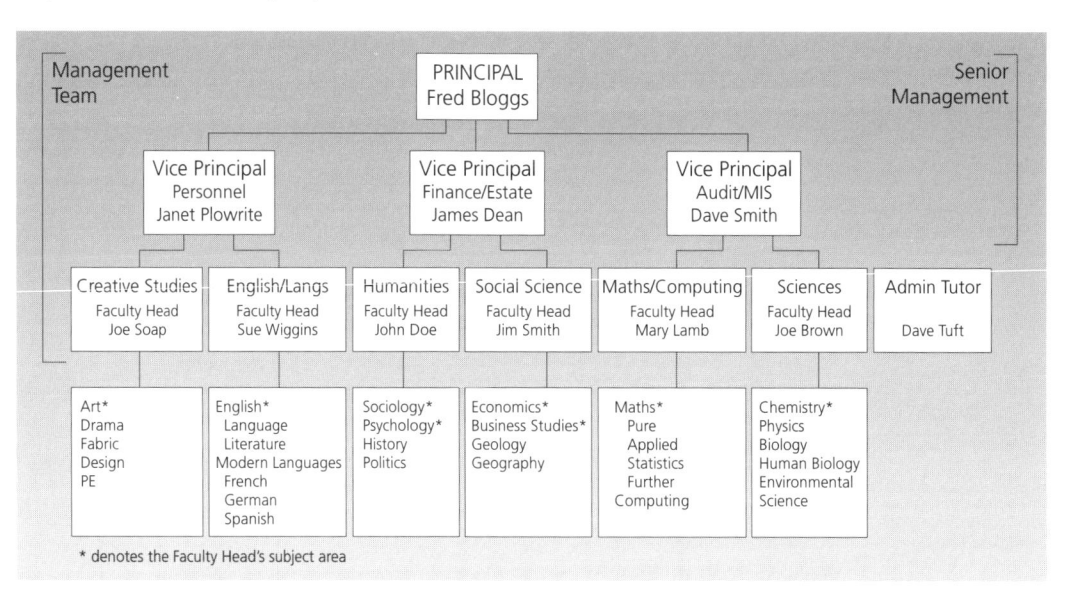

```
Management Team                    PRINCIPAL                         Senior Management
                                   Fred Bloggs

        Vice Principal          Vice Principal          Vice Principal
        Personnel               Finance/Estate          Audit/MIS
        Janet Plowrite          James Dean              Dave Smith

Creative Studies  English/Langs  Humanities   Social Science  Maths/Computing  Sciences      Admin Tutor
Faculty Head      Faculty Head   Faculty Head Faculty Head    Faculty Head     Faculty Head  Dave Tuft
Joe Soap          Sue Wiggins    John Doe     Jim Smith       Mary Lamb        Joe Brown

Art*              English*       Sociology*   Economics*      Maths*           Chemistry*
Drama             Language       Psychology*  Business Studies* Pure           Physics
Fabric            Literature     History      Geology         Applied          Biology
Design            Modern Languages Politics   Geography       Statistics       Human Biology
PE                French                                      Further          Environmental
                  German                                      Computing        Science
                  Spanish
```

* denotes the Faculty Head's subject area

Figure 20 Sixth-form college: management structure of teaching staff

- *Can you spot any communication problems?*
- *If I am a geography teacher, who are above me in the chain of command?*

- The **chain of command** is down the structure. The more levels in the hierarchy, the longer the chain.
- The **span of control** is how many people a manager has under him/her. A narrow span allows closer supervision, a wider span gives more control to subordinates.

Authority and responsibility

Authority can be delegated (i.e. given) to a subordinate. For example, a head of department could authorise a member of staff to buy some books, but the head is still responsible if anything goes wrong.

Authority is the ability to carry out a task, the manager has the **responsibility** to see it is done.

Line authority is the vertical authority seen in the above diagram.

Staff authority is when there is a cross-college role, e.g. IT co-ordinator, who has input into many areas, usually in an advisory role only.

Centralisation *vs* decentralisation

- Centralised, senior management have more control, more standardisation – but might be stressful for senior managers.
- Decentralisation
  - gives subordinates more job satisfaction and uses their local knowledge
  - means quicker decision-making, no need to pass decisions up and down the chain of command
  - makes it easier to groom replacements by delegation of authority.

Other structures

Entrepreneurial

- Central decisions by one or two key members – especially small businesses.

Pyramid/bureaucratic

- The traditional structure for medium and large businesses.

Matrix

- People organised into project teams, e.g. college team for careers.

Factors influencing structure:

- size of business
- views of leaders
- business objectives
- technology changes, e.g. IT reducing administration.

Popular area for questions.

Extension topic 10 Organisational structure

1. What is meant by the term 'chain of command'?

2. How does the 'chain of command' affect the communication system in a business? Consider length of the chain or breadth of span.

3. What are the advantages and disadvantages of having a centralised management structure?

4. What factors might influence the choice of management structure for a business?

5. Binx Chemicals have a fairly traditional management structure, but need to reorganise with more project teams and a flatter structure. What effect might these changes have on communications in the company?

Look at the flow of information in the structure.

ORGANISATIONAL STRUCTURE 63

Extension topic 11

Information systems and organisations

The difference between an information system and a data processing system

- **An information system** is the mechanism which an organisation uses to collect data to help to improve its performance. For example, keeping the names and telephone numbers of business contacts on a sheet of paper which is regularly updated and handed to sales staff would constitute an 'information system'.

- Information technology represents a range of machines which automate the collection of data and help to turn it into useful business information.

- The employment of computers and allied technology will not of itself constitute an information system.

- The existence of an information system is necessary for an organisation's survival. The technology will allow a business to exploit the properties of the system more readily.

An MIS might consist of something more than information technology and electronic data gathering. In fact it includes all means – voice, paper memoranda, written reports and electronically gathered intelligence – of providing relevant information about a business's performance on which management might make informed decisions.

Data processing is (usually):

an electronic means of carrying out fairly routine and repetitive business activities such as

- stock control
- payroll calculations
- invoicing
- counting goods at a supermarket check-out.

Note difference between IS and data processing.

The role and relevance of an information system in aiding decision-making

Management require relevant and timely information which aids decision-making in the business.
Relevant information is information which:

- increases knowledge
- reduces uncertainty in the field of decision-making
- is helpful/useable for a specific purpose.

Managers need information, but not necessarily the same information. The style and quantity of the required information depend on the role and position of the manager in the company's management structure:

At an operational level

- Data processing operations at a day-to-day level produce data, e.g. a supermarket selling bottles of lemonade.

Note the three levels.

64 INFORMATION TECHNOLOGY REVISION NOTES

The data captured will include some of the following elements:

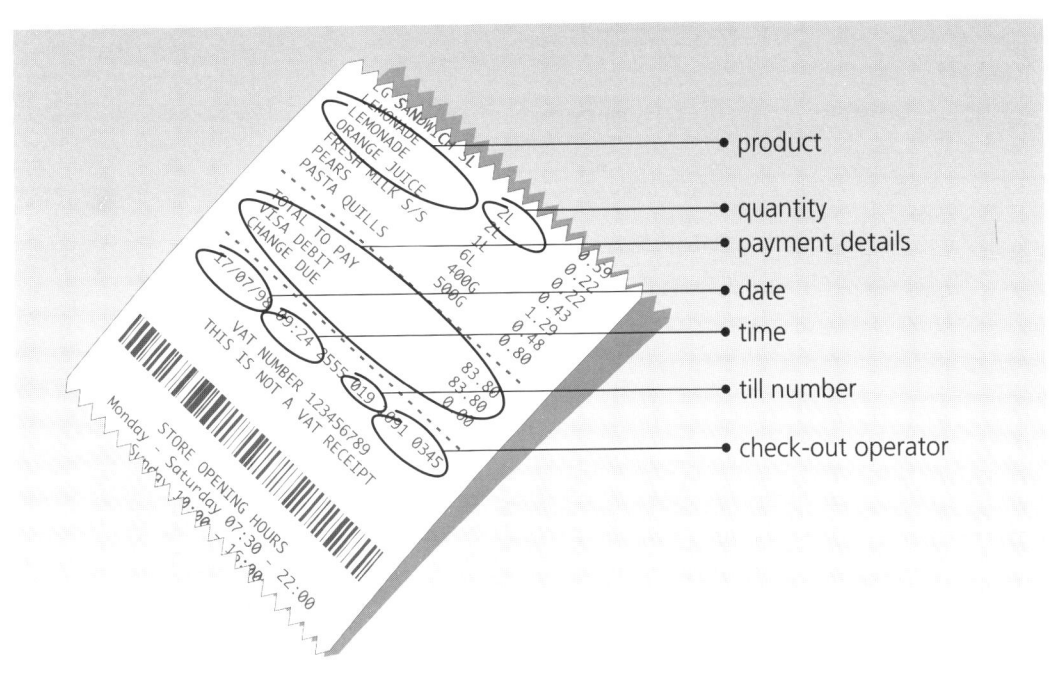

- product
- quantity
- payment details
- date
- time
- till number
- check-out operator

At a tactical level

The data captured above can be processed to yield management information such as:

- total number of bottles of lemonade sold
- number of customers passing through each check-out per hour – therefore efficiency of each check-out operative
- profit.

and can be used to make **tactical decisions**, e.g. move product on shelf, reduce price, give further staff training.

At a strategic level

- At the decision-making level, models and expert systems can be fed the data to produce 'what if' predictions, upon which strategic decisions can be made.
- This level is for the senior management and is often called **decision support**.
- It does not matter at which level the manager is operating, information systems are an aid to decision-making.
- They are not a substitute for decision-making.
- A good manager is not created by a good management information system, but supported by it. It might improve the speed at which a decision is made and give objective credibility to that decision.

The management levels: remember OPTACS – OPerational, TACtical, Strategic.

Extension topic 11 Information systems and organisations

1 Management information systems usually have three different levels. Name and describe each.

2 Distinguish between data processing and an information system.

3 How might a data processing operation become part of an information system?

4 'A management information system supports decision-making – it does not replace it.' To what extent do you agree with this statement?

Extension topic 12: Definition of a management information system

Read these points carefully. Definitions need to be accurate.

Essential characteristics of information

Data needs to be relevant and the processing to be meaningful in order for the information to be of value.

The value of the information itself cannot be guaranteed, but there are certain necessary characteristics of information that must be present if it is to be of assistance to the decision-maker. It must be:

relevant
- The current market price of gas or oil might be a vital piece of information that is used in many decisions, but if it is not of direct relevance to the decision currently under consideration then it is not worth having.

accurate
- If a decision-maker goes to the trouble of identifying some information that will help reduce the uncertainty of a decision, he or she will need to be confident of the accuracy of that information.
- Using an inaccurate figure of 15% for the cost of capital instead of the correct 20% could lead the decision-maker to accept the project mistakenly.

complete
- Once the information necessary to support the decision has been identified, it is essential to process the data to provide a complete set of the information.
- For example, it would be of little use if all the costs except those for the year in question could be provided.
- Absence of current year costs would lead to an incomplete cash flow, therefore invalidating conclusions drawn from the information.

timely
- The information has to be provided at the time that it is required by the decision-maker.
- Many budgetary control systems are ineffective because the information on expenditure can only be produced three months after the expenditure has occurred.

verifiable
- Management might need to justify the decisions that they take.
- For this reason, any decision-maker needs to have confidence in the accuracy and completeness of the information provided.
- It is therefore often desirable for management to be able to verify that the information is sound.

Questions

Extension topic 12 Definition of a management information system

1. a) What is the purpose of a management information system?
   b) Why is such a system required by managers of an organisation?
   c) Give one example of the use of a management information system within an organisation, clearly stating its purpose.

   (NEAB1997)

Extension topic 13

The development and life cycle of an information system

Go for the basic principles – don't get into too much detail.

This simple model has been extensively used for more than 30 years and has given shape to the practices of systems development.

Most methods and techniques used by information system professionals fit one or more of the stages of the life cycle model.

The life cycle is a model used to structure the development process as a sequence of phases.

The names and the number of phases and stages vary, but the fundamental characteristics of the model remain the same.

- The development project begins with the **establishment of clear specifications** of the system to be delivered.
- The development **tasks are put into a logical order** so each completed part leads easily to the next stage.
- The development project **ends with the completion of a system** which is **tested** against the initial specifications.
- This system is then **expected to be used** with minor alterations for a period of time, until the whole process starts over again.

Development of an information system is recognised as a much wider process than just the engineering of computer software. It is not engineering rigour which is valued most, but the ability to manage the long and complex development process.

In support of this, the life cycle provides a simple structure which is easily understood and therefore makes it possible to spread common professional practices, and to generalise from the experience of one project to others.

By following the life cycle, it becomes easier to plan and manage the tasks of systems development. The method provides a pattern which helps in planning the resources required:

- when different activities should take place
- the different people who will be needed and when
- the amounts of financial and computer resources required.

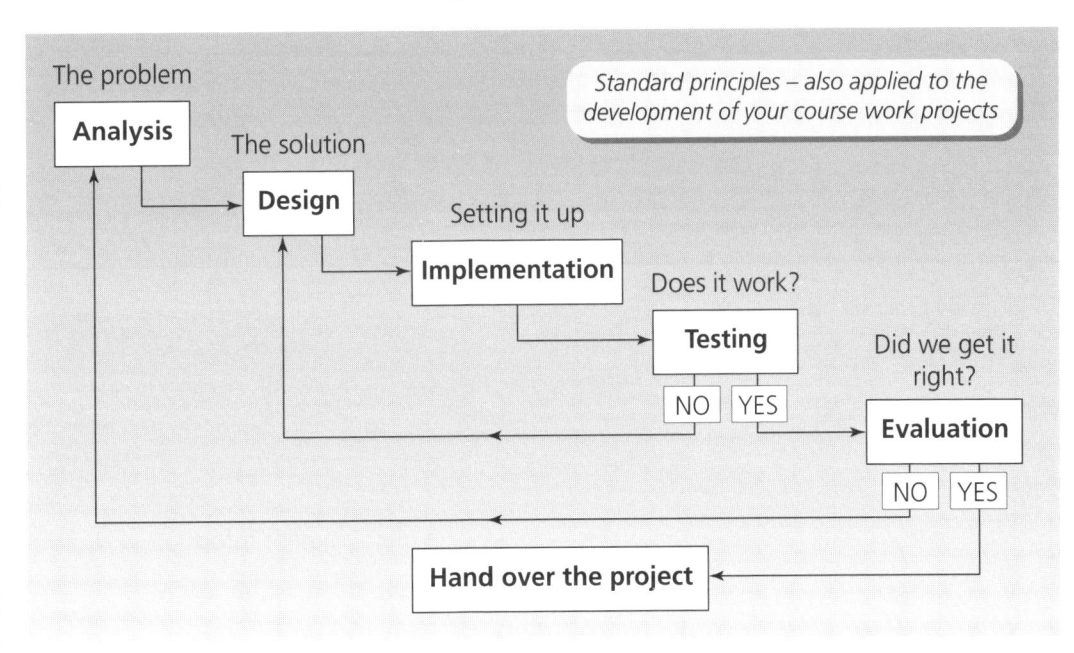

Figure 21 Information system life cycle

Questions

Extension topic 13 The development and life cycle of an information system

1 Discuss the advantages and disadvantages of using the life cycle model as a means of project design and management.

2 Binx Chemicals are considering introducing a range of computer equipment and software to assist with project appraisal. How might the life cycle principles help the company to plan the introduction of this new equipment?

Extension topic 14

Success or failure of a management information system

Precise reasons why failure occurs.

The factors influencing the success or failure of an information system:

- Inadequate analysis – data flows, processing and output have not been assessed correctly.
- Lack of management involvement in design – management has neither understood nor been involved in assessing the system needs.
- Emphasis on computer system – too much time and energy has been given to looking at computer equipment rather than the overall information system.
- Concentration on low-level data processing –
  - Paying employees is a fairly routine data processing activity.
  - The same data – hours worked, overtime hours, days off sick and so on could be used for manpower planning – shift pattern reorganisation for example.
  - The data is being collected once and turned to other purposes.
- Lack of management knowledge of IT systems and their capabilities.
  - Recent surveys have tended to show that IT executives – those responsible for commissioning and paying for IT projects – have mostly come from the realms of accountancy, whilst data process and computer managers are mostly from the technical side.
- Inappropriate/excessive management demands.
  - This point tends to link with the one above, in that a lack of understanding of the capabilities of systems can lead to excessive demands or unrealistic time periods in which to commission new systems.
- Lack of teamwork.
  - Modern systems tend not to be constructed by one person.
  - They are the result of considerable teamwork – system analysts, design engineers, software engineers, project managers and so on.
  - If any one of these fails to deliver their piece of the project then cost over-runs are likely.
- Lack of professional standards.
  - If systems are developed without appropriate standards then they are likely to fail.
  - If staff have not been trained adequately or do not work in an acceptable manner (e.g. no documentation on systems, lack of minutes or decision notes from team meetings), then this is not a recipe for success.

Management involvement a must for success.

Fairly straightforward – but definitions and reasons need to be accurate.

Questions

Think carefully about the role of management in decision-making.

Extension topic 14 Success or failure of a management information system

1 List the major factors which could lead to the successful introduction of a management information system.

2 Successful innovation of a system often needs a 'champion' to carry the project through to its conclusion. How would you define an 'IT champion'? Why do you think such a character would be essential in an IT setting?

3 'Managers need to be brought up to speed regarding IT strategy.' To what extent do you agree with this statement?

Extension topic 15

Information flow

Examples of information flows are helpful – look at flows in your school/college.

The efficient flow of information through an organisation can influence the quality of decision-making within the organisation for the better.

Lack of information, or information that is ill-timed and poorly presented can lead to inappropriate business decisions.

Thus factors influencing information flow might include:

- Organisation structure:
  - the number of levels through which information must flow

- Geographical structure of the organisation:
  - on one site
  - spread over more than one site
  - sites in more than one country

- How data originates within an organisation:
  - point-of-sale terminals
  - process monitoring via data logging
  - handwritten notes/reports

  Electronically gathered.

- Where data originates within an organisation:
  - management surveys/reports
  - operational data logging

- The validity of data:
  - is the data acceptable in the context of the business operation?
  - does the data conform to predetermined standards?

- The preparation and input of data:
  - enough resources have been given to preparation
  - data is available in time for decision-making

- The volume of data to be collected and input:
  - those requiring the processed data are aware/unaware of the size of the task
  - enough resources have been allocated to handle the job

- The processing cycle:
  - the job requirements fit into existing operations of the data processing department

- The specification of reports:
  - clear requirements have been given as to the style and contents of reports

- The report distribution cycle:
  - requirements for reports fit the data processing routine
  - those wanting reports receive them
  - those needing reports receive them

- The report timing cycle:
  - reports are available on time and in line with decision-making requirements

- Formal vs informal requests and responses:
  - a balance exists between formal requests for information – as per company procedures – and informal requests – 'off the cuff' – not according to procedures
  - informal could overtake formal

- Quality of data:
  - data meets the business's standards and is relevant to the needs of decision-making

- The techniques/structure for monitoring and organising the information flow:
  - the flow of data and information needs checking – along with other activities in the business
  - modifications are needed to improve efficiency

Part of audit procedures.

Extension topic 15 Information flow

1 What are the characteristics of good information?

2 Why does poor information flow influence the quality of decision-making in an organisation?

3 What procedures could be put into place to monitor the information flow in an organisation? What action could be taken to improve the flow and effectiveness of the information created?

Audit procedures.

Extension topic 16

Personnel and information systems

In smaller businesses all three functions might be carried out by the same people – they are required no matter the size of the business.

Three major management functions tend to exist in businesses. They are:

- **strategic management**
- **tactical management**
- **organisational management**.

These functions supply to and demand from an MIS different forms of information along with different requirements for software support.

Management level	MIS requirement	Software requirement
Strategic management	Environmental scanning Reporting	Decision support system Modelling Expert systems
Tactical management	Control and monitoring Reporting Exception reporting	Decision support systems Modelling Expert systems
Operational management	Control and monitoring Exception reporting Transaction processing – customers and employees	Optimising models (some decision support systems) Data collection – stock management – payroll processing

Not everyone wants the same type of support.

- **Data**, **summaries**, **reports** and **information** generated at lower levels are passed up the chain of responsibility.
- **Company objectives**, **plans** and **targets** are passed down from senior management to be acted upon tactically and operationally.

Questions

Extension topic 16 Personnel and information systems

1 The manager of a company complains that the management information system (MIS) continually fails to produce the appropriate information at the right time. The person responsible for the MIS responds by blaming the 'inadequate data and information flow' within the company and requests a review of 'data and information flows'.

   (a) State **six** factors which influence the flow of information and data within an organisation.

   (b) With the aid of examples, describe **three techniques** which could be used to review the current information flows.   (NEAB 1997)

Extension topic 17: Developments within management information systems

Decision support systems

- A **management information system** is able to deal with enquiries by the user (such as 'How much will this investment cost over 5 years ?').
- Most of the data required for this enquiry is derived from the operational system and the user only has to supply the parameters of the search, such as – account number, current balance, range of dates.
- There are many problems in management that are not so straightforward and these tend to occur when managers are thinking about strategic or tactical issues.

Such problems can be assisted by **decision support systems** (DSS) which allow the user to partly formulate the problem as he or she proceeds to solve it.

For example, a form on the DSS may be set up, using a spreadsheet package. The user will have some idea of the costs and the benefits of a proposed project, probably derived from parts of the MIS, and will be able to feed them into the system and get a result.

'What if?' questions

- A major requirement in the solution of unstructured problems is the ability to vary some of the parameters of the problem to see the effect on the solution.
- This form of sensitivity analysis is particularly useful in capital investment appraisal.
- Very often the outcome of the analysis (whether or not to invest) hangs on the cost of capital to the firm.
- The firm can borrow capital from a bank or finance house or it can issue more shares in the case of a public company.
- Whichever alternative is chosen, the resulting cost of capital can vary.

A decision support system gives the user the ability to ask 'What if?' (the cost of capital were to increase from 17.46% to 18.21%).

Ease of use

- Most users of decision support systems can best be described as **occasional users**, in that they do not spend the majority of their working day on the DSS.
- Most of the early operational systems were designed for use by **regular users** and there was not a great deal of effort put into the design of the **human–computer interface** (HCI).
- **At best** the users of such systems were confronted with overcrowded screens which were used both to gather input and report results.
- **The worst** HCI consisted of complicated commands that had to be typed in (and memorised).
- Early attempts at MIS development used these operational systems as a building platform, consequently they were either extremely difficult or over-cumbersome to use.
- A complicated HCI can be mastered, but only if the user accesses it on a regular basis, when the command sequences or the routes to particular screens become firmly fixed in the memory.

- These difficulties in HCIs contributed to the early disillusionment with MISs and led to the drive towards the development of better interfaces.

A **DSS** requires **an easy-to-use (user-friendly) HCI**. Most contemporary DSSs use either:

- a menu system or
- a window-icon-mouse pointer (WIMP) system.

Another important feature that the DSS must possess is a **fast response to requests** or commands that are input to the system.

Interactive use of a system is a series of stimulus and response events, separated by time gaps. These time gaps can be categorised as thinking time (by the user) and the machine equivalent response time.

Human expectations of computers have developed along with the speed of the machines. This has led to:

- a design parameter of **a maximum response time of two seconds** becoming the normal guideline in the industry
- an average response of one half-second appears to be quite acceptable in pseudo real-time operational systems used for business or commercial purposes.

It must be noted, however, that the response time is dictated by the needs of the application.

Graphical output

DSSs are often used as part of strategic or tactical planning or decision-making and there is often the requirement for the user to be able to present complex information quickly and concisely in order to get a 'feel' for a particular problem.

Integrated database and query language

This is more a question of system architecture (the structure of the system) than a feature for users.

- In order to provide most of the facilities described above, the DSS should be built around **a relational database**.
- The extraction is performed by the database management system and the user is able to put requests to the system using a set of instructions known as a query language.

As well as the ability to set up and manipulate their own databases, **it is essential** that:

- DSSs have access to the corporate databases
- data can be extracted and imported to the internal DSS database for further manipulation.

Executive information systems (EISs)

(also known as executive support systems)

EISs are clearly aimed at the strategic level of planning and decision-making.

They share all the features of decision support systems in particular:

- ease of use
- fast response
- ability to generate graphical output
- built on (usually) relational database systems accessed indirectly through a query language
- access to the corporate databases.

Since strategic planning involves the consideration of alternative scenarios or views of the future, it is essential for the EIS to provide (and extend) the 'What if?' facilities described under DSSs.

Alternative views of the information

Scenario planning involves looking at corporate-wide plans and decisions in a particular future environment.

To do this the executive will need to look at the information relating to each aspect of the operation from a different perspective or in greater detail.

This activity of gradually increasing the level of detail but decreasing the scope is known as 'drilling down'.

Questions

Extension topic 17 Developments within management information systems

1 What characteristics are usually associated with executive information systems? What benefits would such a system bring to a company's senior managers?

2 In what category of information system would you place a spreadsheet-based application? Explain your choice.

3 Describe four categories of software that you would expect to find as part of a company's office automation system.

4 A range of software packages can be described as 'Project management software'. What is project management software and what does it do?

(NEAB Specimen Questions 1996)

Extension topic 18

Corporate information systems strategy

Vague definitions are unacceptable – note the list.

Factors influencing the structure of a MIS

There are a number of factors which influence the style and structure of a company's management information system:

Factors connected to the Management information system:
- Business structure
- Main business function
- Management style
- Range of business decisions
- Business monitoring and control
- Information technology
- National and international government
- Legal framework
- Environment

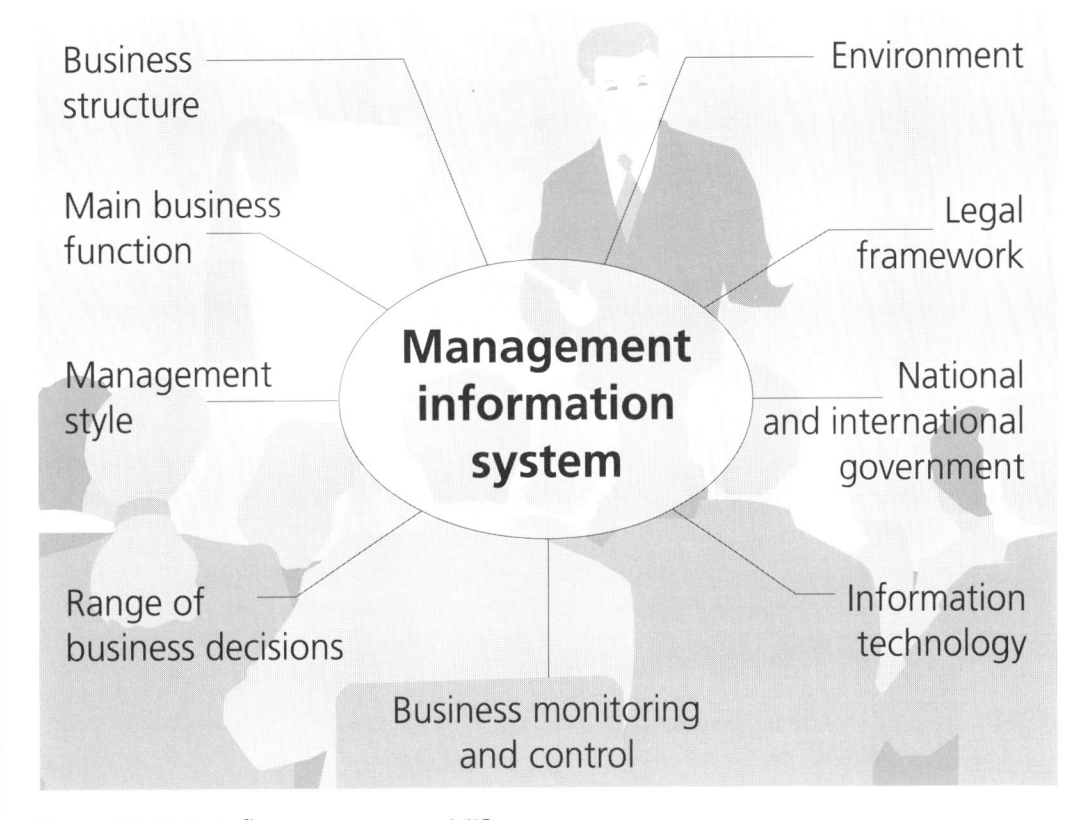

Figure 22 Main influences upon an MIS

Range of business decisions
- What decisions does the business need to take in order to carry out its function?
- Do business decisions need to be taken quickly on a day-to-day basis?

Information technology
- To what extent does the business already use IT?
- What training will be required?
- What expertise is there in the business?
- What equipment is available and what will need to be added?

Management style
- To what extent is management centralised?
- To what extent are others allowed to participate in management?
- To what extent are management functions closely defined and monitored?

Business monitoring and control
- To what extent is planning a formal activity?
- Which levels of management are involved in controlling the business?
- What data and information is required to check the efficiency of the business?

CORPORATE INFORMATION SYSTEMS STRATEGY 77

Main business function
- In which sector is the business operating – raw materials, manufacturing or financial services?
- What demands are placed on the business from operating in the sector?

Business structure
- What is the size of the operation?
- How many people are employed?
- What is the geographical distribution of the assets?

Legal framework
- What are the legal requirements of operating in the chosen sector?
- What are the general business requirements?

National and international governments
- How does the business deal with the requirements of government?
- To what information does it need to respond?

The environment
- To what extent is external information important to the business?
- How does it obtain such information?
- What relationships does it have with customers, clients, suppliers and competitors?

Other influences on the structure and future development of an MIS might include:

Personalities of employees –
- whether or not there is sufficient understanding of information systems amongst managers and the managed
- whether or not an 'IT champion' emerges who can enthuse over the need for MIS development.

Motivation
- whether employees are sufficiently motivated to use a system effectively and to support its development
- whether or not they feel 'involved' in change and its specification.

Ability to adapt to change
- whether employees are able to cope with very sophisticated systems
- whether management is willing to help employees cope.

An MIS should suit each part of the business function and should respond to management needs.

For example, Production Management might require precise measurement and feedback systems leading to fairly tight control of operations.

Research and development might be less clearly defined and might not lend itself to precise control; after all the researchers might not have anything to control – yet!

A very centralised management structure, where the spread of responsibility is severely limited, will mean there is much demand for information to be passed up the chain of command with instructions and guidance coming down.

A decentralised system implies greater autonomy for departments and wider spread of responsibility. There is a need to share information between managers at the same level. The amount of information being passed up the chain of command is much reduced.

Questions

Extension topic 18 Corporate information systems strategy

1 What are the major factors influencing the structure of a company's management information system?

2 Why is it important for a company to develop an information systems strategy? How might it go about preparing such a strategy?

Extension topic 19

Expert systems and artificial intelligence

Note definition given here.

'Intelligent systems' is the new term being used for real-world uses of artificial intelligence. AI is a group of technologies that attempt to copy certain aspects of human behaviour, such as :

- reasoning
- communicating
- mimicking our senses.

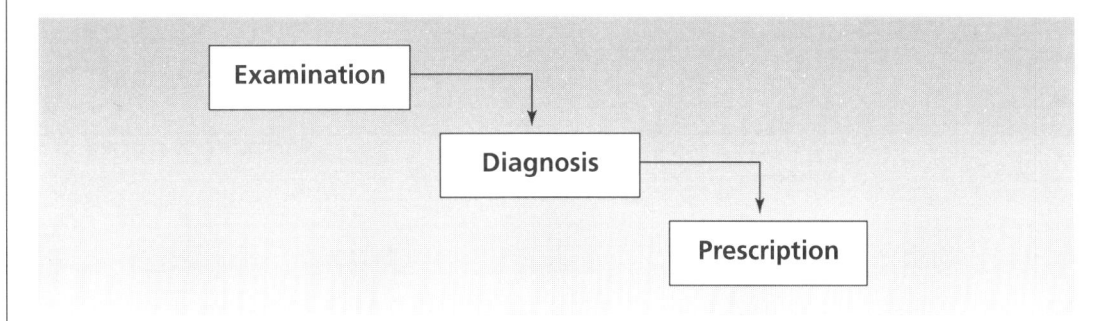

Examination → Diagnosis → Prescription

Figure 23 Expert system. 'Trust me, I'm a doctor.'

What is an expert system?

- A type of **problem-solving** model, almost always implemented on a computer, that deals with a problem the way an 'expert', such as a doctor or lawyer, does.

- The solution process involves consulting a base of knowledge or expertise to reason out an answer based on the characteristics of the problem.

An **expert system** should be able to:

- solve a problem
- explain to some extent how it solved that problem
- provide a reliable means of solving similar problems.

Components of expert systems

There are **three components** in an expert system:

- a user interface
- an inference engine
- a knowledge base.

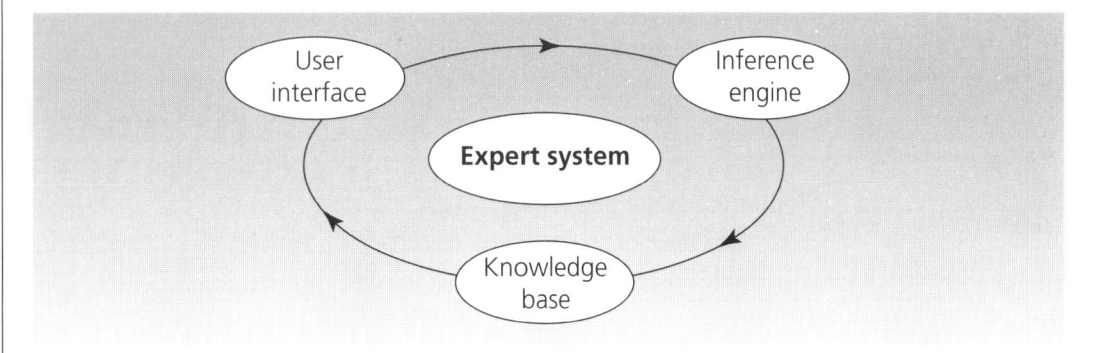

Figure 24 Expert system

The user interface is the interface between the expert system and outside world.

The user interface can be:

- a simple menu
- an ordinary word-processing screen
- a database form
- a spreadsheet screen
- a multimedia link.

The inference engine is that part of the software that contains the reasoning methods used to search the knowledge base.

- The expert system generally asks questions of the user to get the information it needs.
- The inference engine, using the knowledge base, searches for the sought-after knowledge and returns a decision or recommendation to the user.
- A knowledge base contains facts and data relevant to a specific application. The inference engine uses this information to reason out the problem.

Uses of expert systems

- Case-based reasoning (CBR) is a recently popular form of knowledge representation in expert systems, arriving on the market in 1991.
- These systems compare a current problem (or case) with hundreds or thousands of similar past cases and look at possible treatments or outcomes.
- Case-based reasoning is best used when the situation involves too many variations to be generalised into rules.

Case study: Apache III

Apache III is an expert system used by intensive-care units in the USA. Thus, when a thirty-five year old woman entered a Michigan hospital with a potentially fatal respiratory disease, the medical staff in the intensive care unit entered her details into Apache III. The system drew on the records of 17,448 previous intensive-care patients to predict whether she would live or die. Its first prediction was that she had a 16 per cent chance of dying.

Her details were entered daily and the system compared her progress to the base of previous cases. Two weeks later, her chance of dying had risen to 90 per cent, alerting the doctors to take corrective action. Then, literally overnight, her chance of dying dropped to 60 per cent, and twelve days later to 40 percent. By the end of the month she had recovered.

The system is able to monitor progress very closely, thus helping staff to note improvement or decline faster than it might have been noted in the past. So the system is helping units respond faster and to control costs more effectively.

There are many uses for CBR, including:

- answering questions at a help desk
- matching job requirements to job candidates
- selecting pre-prepared letters to reply to incoming letters
- finding legal precedents
- identifying code modules for reuse.

Look out for other examples!

Fuzzy logic

- Fuzzy logic is an AI technology that allows computers to handle precisely concepts and fuzzy notions, such as tall, warm, cool, good, near, far, and so on.
- It allows a computer system to work more closely to the way people talk and think.
- Fuzzy logic simplifies complexity; therefore, it is very useful for controlling very complex systems or situations.
- Fuzzy logic is being widely used in consumer products – auto focus cameras, lifts, washing machines, underground trains, and so forth – because it allows smoother operation of machines and appliances.

Uses of expert systems

Although expert systems are playing an increasing role in company operations, three specific uses come to mind:

- to assist knowledge workers
- for competitive purposes – to deal directly with customers
- to augment conventional systems.

Questions

Extension topic 19 Expert systems and artificial intelligence

1 What are the characteristics of an expert system?

2 In what circumstances would managers use an expert system?

3 What are the dangers of relying too heavily on expert systems to aid decision-making?

Core topic 17: Capabilities and limitations of IT systems

VARCS!
Volume
accuracy
repetition
complexity
speed.

The main reasons IT systems are introduced are:

- **volume**: large amount of data is being stored/retrieved and updated (1 filing cabinet = 1 CD ROM)
- **accuracy**: the processing required accuracy
- **repetition**: data is processed in a repetitive manner
- **complexity**: data has to be processed in ways that are not possible manually, e.g. searching, selecting, combining to provide information
- **speed**: data needs to be processed quickly enough to provide information that can affect the input, i.e. FEEDBACK, e.g. point of sales ordering.

There are **limitations** to what IT systems can do.

For example, a major bank wanted to introduce a cheque scanning system that would scan a cheque, do optical character recognition and store the resulting scan. On doing the sums it was found it would have taken 30 hours to process one day's cheques, so the idea was abandoned.

This was an example of **technical or hardware limitation**. Other examples might be:

- the processor is too slow for the task demanded of it
- the hard disk can't retrieve data quickly enough
- the printer resolution is too low so the pictures look grainy.

Sometimes the **software has limits**, e.g.

- a database reaches the limit of possible files open in DOS
- a database can only hold a certain maximum number of fields in a record
- a spreadsheet can only contain a certain number of cells.

Other limitations might affect the system but not be immediately apparent, e.g. a communications system could be too slow for what you wish to do, e.g. the Internet is very slow when the USA is awake.

Other limitations exist:
If a database is designed incorrectly, it may not be possible to extract the required information. E.g. if the address field also included the post code (i.e. no separate post code) then grouping the records according to post code would be a problem.

Questions

Core topic 17 Capabilities and limitations of IT systems

1 Name and describe three features of a non-computerised system that might make it advantageous to introduce a computerised system.

2 Describe a situation you have studied where the introduction of an IT system has not been carried out due to the limitations of that system.

3 Describe some typical limitations an IT system might possess.

4 The introduction of an IT system has produced no advantages over the previous manual system. How could this happen?

Extension topic 20: The management of change

Information systems executives now realise that line managers play an important role in the successful implementation of IT because they can help to develop or kill a new system by their support or resistance.

Potential 'woolly' answers here – note points carefully.

As the use of distributed systems spreads, the responsibility for the correct use of IT will shift to line managers.

- They will need to become familiar with the risks and problems of new systems in their organisation.
- They will also need to ensure that the job, health, and safety needs of their subordinates are being met by a new system.
- They will need to understand the differences between a traditional work environment and one where computers play an important part.
- They will need to be able to manage the transition from old to new.

The management of change is the process of assisting people to make major changes in their working environment.

The management of change has often not been handled methodically, so choosing a suitable methodology and training managers to use it are the first steps toward successfully introducing new computer systems.

A possible approach might include:

- describing the change
- assessing the sponsors' commitment to the project
- evaluating the support or resistance of the targets
- assessing the change agents' skills.

The purpose of these initial evaluations is to determine whether the change can be made successfully with the current **scope**, **sponsors**, **change agents**, and **targets**. By evaluating each area, the change agent can see where more education or a new approach is needed to make the project more likely to succeed.

Case study: Swift's Bank

Swift's Bank has one hundred branches throughout the country and a large computer-communication network connecting these branches. In the financial services field, managing change has become an increasingly important talent especially where new computer systems are concerned.

To teach the bank's managers to manage change better, the company bought in a course entitled 'How to Manage Change in Organisations,' which is taught by the bank's own staff.

The course raises employees' awareness of change and how it can be managed. Issues such as the uses and misuses of power, resistance to change, acceptance of change and commitment to change are covered. Course members also learn about the roles people play in a change process – sponsor, agent of change and target.

The course graduates leave with an organisational change planning kit that they can use on their own whenever they plan a major change project.

[continued on next page]

The bank includes this change management approach in its system development procedures. Once a manager has assessed the readiness for change, project teams work on managing the problems they have uncovered. They involve users as much as possible in system development to ensure that when the system is installed, the users will feel that they are its owners.

Think about these issues

1 In the context of managing change what is meant by the following terms
   a) sponsors   b) change agents   c) targets?

2 Why did the bank need to manage change?

3 What are the likely effects of change in a business for:
   a) The operations staff?   b) Executive management?

4 Why is it important to plan for change in a business and especially to plan the changes to the information system?

Questions

Extension topic 20 The management of change

1 An information system was introduced into an organisation and was considered a failure. The failure was due to the inability of the organisation to manage the change rather than technical reasons.

With the aid of examples, describe **three** factors which influence the management of change within an organisation.
(NEAB 1997)

Extension topic 21

Audit requirements

Information technology systems are subject to audit in exactly the same way as hand-written systems.

The role of the auditor is to check that systems operate correctly and deliver the expected results.

By following the procedure shown in the diagram an auditor ought to be able to discover whether or not the system is working and the records of payments tie up with the records of claims. The system ought to be tight enough to prevent fraudulent claims.

Remember auditing is not confined to finance – it deals with all procedures.

Your security is only as good as the weakest link!

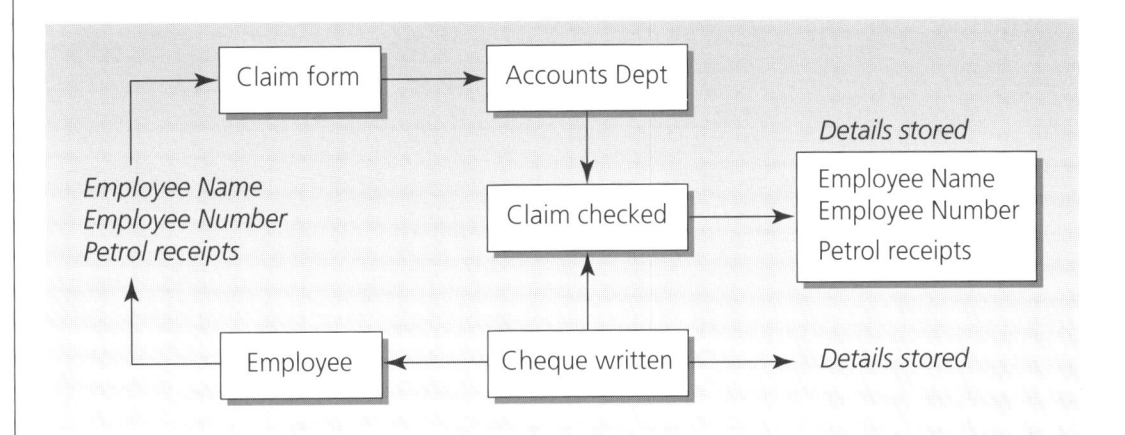

Figure 25 Sample audit trail for travel expenses

If this is not the case then the auditor will recommend changes which ought to secure the system.

Sometimes the system will work, but give the wrong results.

- This may be the result of a transcription error.
- Additional checking might be recommended to manage this item.

It is the responsibility of the auditor to determine whether or not an organisation's assets are properly protected.

When a manual data processing system has been properly developed and is being operated efficiently, the auditor's task is a fairly straightforward one.

- Procedures are well documented.
- Hard copies of all transactions are available.
- An audit trail can be followed.
- Duties will be separated so as to minimise the possibility of collusion and fraud.

Written procedures are no good without physical checks.

But when data processing is carried out electronically, special problems are faced by an auditor:

- The auditor may lack knowledge of computer terms and concepts.

- The computer personnel responsible for developing the new systems may know little about accountancy or audit.

- Data processing can lead to centralisation. This means that one traditional safeguard against error and fraud – the principle of the segregation of duties – is lost, because the computer carries out all the required tasks.

As computer processing is automatic, human, common-sense checks cannot easily be built into the system.

An audit trail will be difficult to follow when processing is computerised.

- Data within a computer system is invisible to the human being.
- Many computer systems, in order to reduce processing costs, do not hold historical data in the way that many manual systems do.
- The vast majority of transactions may not be printed out.

The 'exception principle' – I only print what I need.

Real-time systems pose special problems:

- As data originates at remote locations, transactions are more difficult to check, and, problems are increased when, for example, orders received over the telephone are input directly to a computer system without a hard copy being made.
- Unauthorised use of the terminal can also cause difficulties.
- Problems arise when the pseudo real-time system fails whilst transactions are being dealt with.

Did I update the master file?

In particular, the auditors must verify:

- the design of the system is sound
- the day-to-day running of the system is being properly carried out.

Several steps can be taken by the auditor in an attempt to overcome the special problems posed by computerised data processing systems.

- It is useful for at least one member of an audit team to have extensive first-hand experience of computing.
- A good working relationship must be established with the computer department's personnel.
- The auditors must take an active role, rather than a passive one, when a new system is being developed, or an existing system is being modified.

An audit trail can be created where one does not already exist. This will allow the auditors to check that transactions are correctly actioned.

Standard audit packages are available which:

- allow random sampling of the contents of the file, perhaps printing every nth. record
- cause exceptional items to be printed
- give control totals for certain important fields. Where such packages are not available, they can be written internally.
- Spot checks on the computer installation, and on certain systems which run on the computer, should be made.
- Questionnaires and checklists can be used by the auditors to ensure that all aspects of control are covered.
- Throughout the work, the auditors must ask questions. Experience will often allow them to sense whether something is wrong with the system.

Questions

Extension topic 21 Audit requirements

1 What is meant by the following terms 'audit' and 'audit trail'?

2 Why is it important to have a 'separation of responsibilities' especially when dealing with computer-based financial management?

3 Why must a business have agreed procedures for accessing and changing data files?

4 If software has built-in audit trail facilities, give five details which you think are essential to demonstrate that the computer files are being used correctly and by authorised personnel.

Extension topic 22: Disaster recovery management

Try and offer examples of problems to support answers.

A business which is highly dependent upon a computer system becomes very vulnerable if the system fails.

- Each possible failure can have some form of back-up or some form of protection, but each additional step taken to secure the system adds to the cost of management.
- Whether or not the decision is taken to add security depends on what is described as the risk potential.

Data is a valuable asset. Look after it.

For example: if there is no risk of losing power to the system, then it is a waste of resources adding a back-up power supply. However, if the risk of power loss is considerable then it would be foolish not to tackle this problem by adding a standby power supply.

Points to consider in the above example:

- How long on average is power down?
- What happens to the data when power is lost?
- How quickly can the system recover when power returns?
- What are the costs to the business of power loss – orders unprocessed, staff frustration, etc.?
- What is the cost of installing a back-up power supply?
- Do the financial losses to the business outweigh the costs of back-up installation?

Risk analysis!

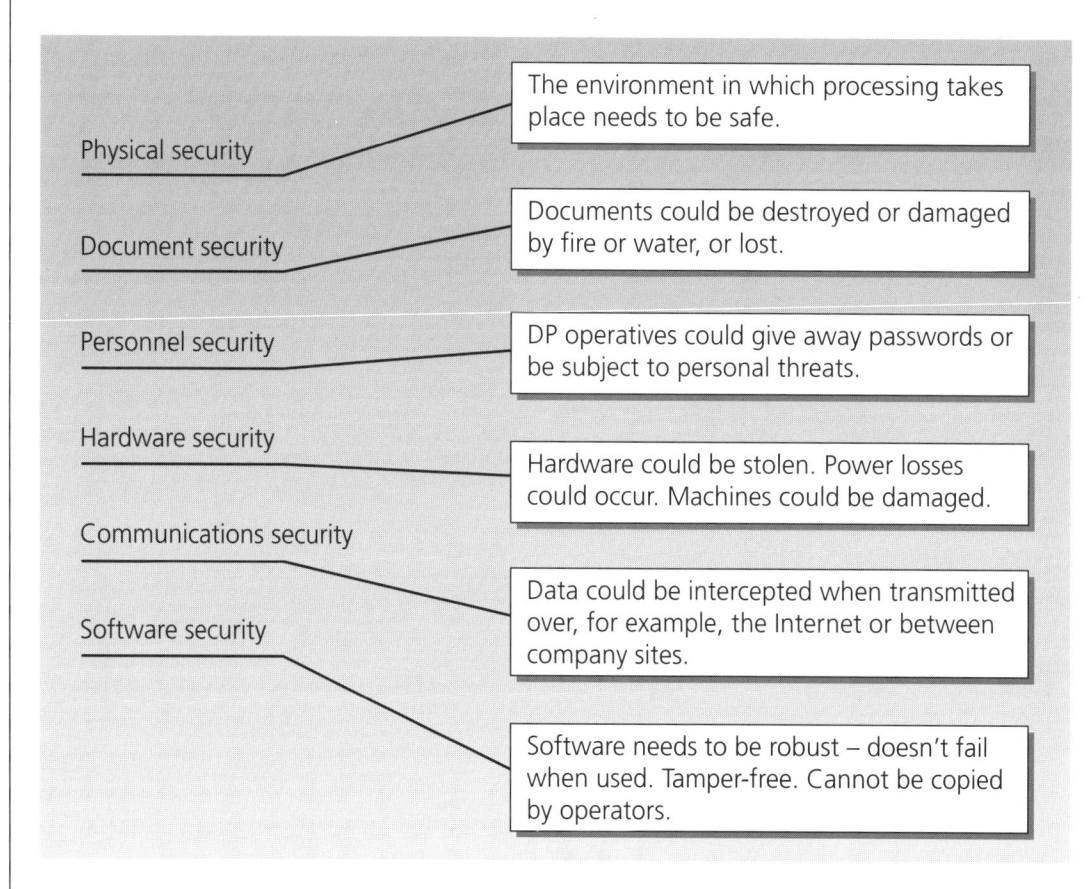

Physical security	The environment in which processing takes place needs to be safe.
Document security	Documents could be destroyed or damaged by fire or water, or lost.
Personnel security	DP operatives could give away passwords or be subject to personal threats.
Hardware security	Hardware could be stolen. Power losses could occur. Machines could be damaged.
Communications security	Data could be intercepted when transmitted over, for example, the Internet or between company sites.
Software security	Software needs to be robust – doesn't fail when used. Tamper-free. Cannot be copied by operators.

Figure 26 Problem areas

Recovery strategy

Flavour your recovery mix with a spoonful of common sense!

Once problems have occurred, solutions must be found.

- Whilst a computer system is out of action or under-performing, the company could be losing money and the confidence of customers.
- Problems have got to be planned for, based upon knowledge of the best working practice in the IT industry. For example, important file servers must not be linked to a power supply which is easily switched off!

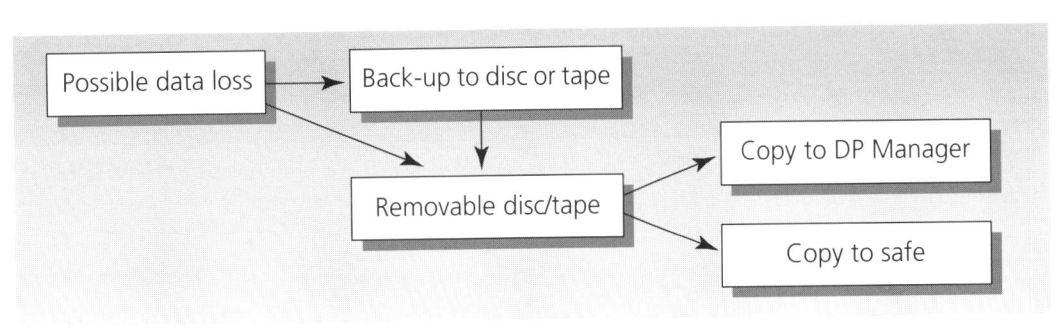

Figure 27 Disaster recovery – potential data loss

Figure 27 illustrates a strategy designed to cope with potential data loss. The key to success here is to make sure adequate **back-ups** are taken and that these are safely stored, preferably not together and not on the same site.

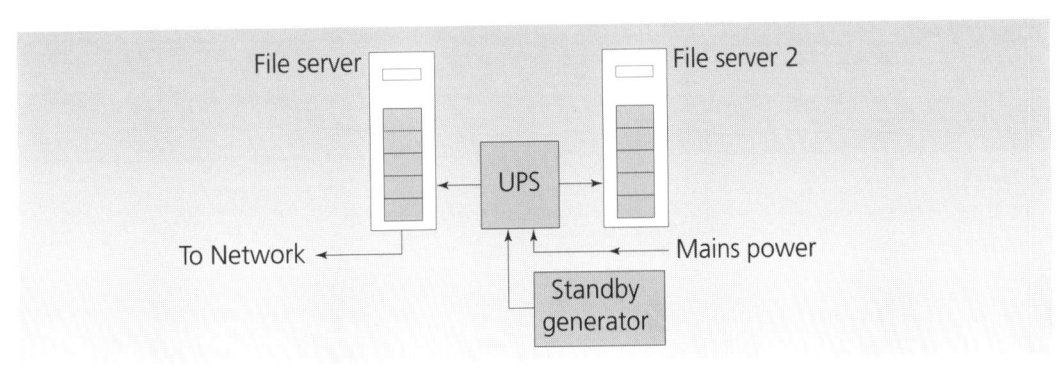

Figure 28 Disaster recovery – power loss

Figure 28 illustrates the situation where two file servers are linked together on a fairly large network. They take their main power from the national grid and it is fed to the file servers through an uninterruptible power supply (UPS).

- A UPS is a sealed battery unit which, when power is lost, detects the loss and switches to the battery.
- This will allow enough time to shut down the file servers safely, to await the restoration of the grid supply or to allow time to start the standby generators.

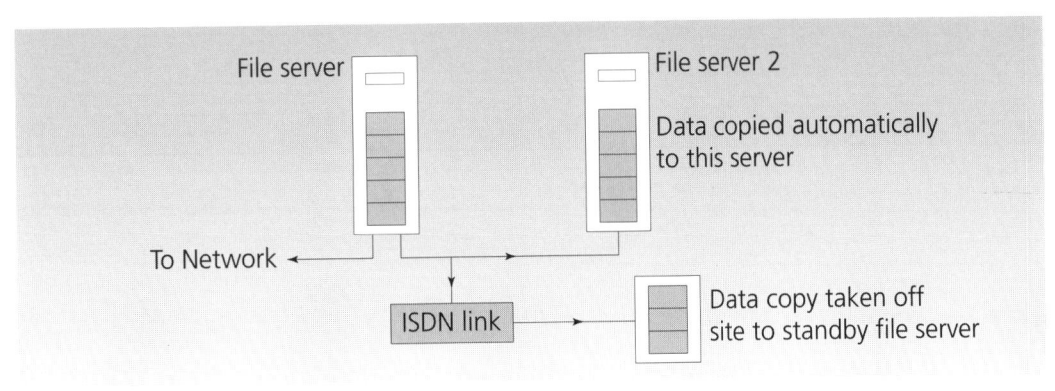

Figure 29 Disaster recovery–machine breakdown

DISASTER RECOVERY MANAGEMENT 89

Figure 29 illustrates a situation where back-up copies are made to both on-site and off-site locations. In both cases a reserve file server is kept ready to use within an hour or so of the main server hitting problems. Where off-site data recording is being done, this might be at the company's service centre or it might be at a service contractor's premises.

In the latter case the service contractor has agreed to keep a file server to the same specification as the one used on the customer's site, loaded with the customer's data for use in the eventuality of a breakdown. The new server can either be delivered to the customer or the data can be used via the fast ISDN link.

No matter what the situation a clear plan of action is required. For example: what happens if there is a breakdown and the DP manager is away? Who takes charge and initiates the recovery procedure?

Questions

Extension topic 22 Disaster recovery management

1 What is a disaster recovery plan? Why is it important for a company to have such a plan?

2 Write a report to your department head setting out the arguments for a carefully managed disaster management and recovery programme.

Core Topic 18: Security, the Data Protection Act and EU Directives

The hardware/software/data need to be part of the strategy.

Security

When an organisation sets up an information systems strategy, one of the concerns should be the security of the systems, data and information that they hold.

Consideration should be given to protection against:

- the physical loss or damage to hardware, software, the network, or data
- protection against unauthorised copying or viewing of the data or software
- protection against unauthorised amendment to the data or software.

Physical security

Physical security is concerned with the security measures taken at, for example, a company's national data centre and at the individual sites where IT is used.

- Loss or damage can occur as a result of **natural disaster** (most commonly equipment malfunction, fire or water damage) or as a result of **deliberate action** to steal or sabotage the equipment.

- To protect against natural disaster it is wise to seek the advice of computer equipment manufacturers, building services professionals and fire safety officers, and there are a number of obvious precautions that can be taken.

- Adequate cover for maintenance in the event of equipment malfunction is essential, as discussed above.

- One 'natural disaster' that is particularly difficult to protect against is the increasing instance of network cables being severed as a result of road or other building works.

- The range of possible acts of sabotage, including theft of equipment, is large, especially in view of the portability of much of today's IT equipment.

- The only really effective defence is to keep would-be perpetrators at bay by using a **'sentry' system**. This form of security can be either:
  - manual (in the form of security guards) or
  - electronic (in the form of security locks or panels on doors).

  It is designed to restrict access to all or parts of the site to authorised personnel only.

- Although it is often an effective deterrent, especially against the opportunist thief, the sentry system is by no means foolproof.

- A determined individual or group of individuals will always be able to by-pass the system either:
  - by forgery of pass or entry cards, or
  - by passing through automatic systems in parallel with authorised users (known as 'tailgating') or, in the extreme case,
  - by physical assault on the staff or the building.

- The main elements of a strategy for physical security will involve procedures for direct protection of the equipment, such as:
  - chaining it down
  - alarm systems
  - lockable doors/cupboards and so on.

- Of equal, if not greater importance, however, are procedures to ensure that **adequate back-ups of data and software are regularly taken**.

- Should any elements of the hardware, system software or the network be damaged, be stolen or malfunction, the provision of adequate back-up will enable the system to be restored as effectively as possible without the loss of valuable data or information.

Security from unauthorised copying/viewing

- Another form of theft from a computer-based system is the copying or viewing of data or software.

- Software, data and information are often one of the most valuable resources of an organisation.

- Information on performance, services, clients, projects and so on would be extremely valuable to a competitor organisation. Failure to secure it would also (in the case of client information) contravene the Data Protection Act.

- In order to steal in this way the thief will require access to the system. In the days of centralised batch processing, security against such access was covered by the provision of physical security.

- Nowadays, however, systems involving multi-access to local and wide area networks have a multitude of vulnerable points where the system can be hacked.

- Password protection can be an effective way of preventing unauthorised access to the complete system or to individual software or databases.

- Various forms of password protection are available including:
  - the simple single password
  - systems that ask for different specific characters from the password each time the system is accessed (such as the third and fifth characters)
  - systems that ask for one from a list of passwords (such as the second from an authorised list of five)
  - systems asking a random series of questions based on the particular user (such as date of birth, mother's maiden name and so on).

In all cases, the aim is to check the validity of the user via a key that only she or he should know.

Most users are extremely lax when using a password system, creating obvious security breaches such as:

- writing the password down in an accessible place
- telling it to colleagues
- speaking the letters as they type them in.

These lapses in secure usage invalidate the common measures taken by systems designers to protect passwords such as blanking them from the screen.

If the thief manages to evade the physical security measures and the password to access the system, there is still a **further level of protection** that can be applied.

- Under most systems the owner or creator of a software file or database is allowed to specify various levels of protection to restrict access to an individual or a small group of users.

- This protection ranges from allowing read-only access to the file to full password protection of the file.

Further security against unauthorised access can be provided by the use of **encryption**.

- Disguising the data by encryption can prove a deterrent to the would-be intruder since it is very difficult to break modern coding systems.

Security from unauthorised amendment

There is another **rapidly growing area** of computer crime.

- This is theft or fraud by the unauthorised manipulation of software or data held on a computer-based system.
- The financial-based systems used by, for example, a firm of accountants would be particularly attractive to this kind of thief and their protection is therefore of the utmost importance.
- Much computer crime of this nature remains unreported (even if it is discovered) due to the fact that public revelation of a major breach of security could seriously undermine public and customer confidence in the organisation.

However, by manipulating data or software the perpetrator can steal by:

- manipulation of foreign currency accounts to take personal advantage from changes in currency rates
- manipulation of inventory systems to arrange for goods to be delivered to bogus customers
- recording bogus payments from those bogus customers
- manipulation of payroll systems to pay fictitious people
- generating false claims on insurance policies.

There are many other variations on these themes.

- To protect against a person from outside the organisation committing these crimes, the measures discussed above would be appropriate as part of the overall security strategy.
- Many of these forms of computer crime are perpetrated by 'insiders' – employees of the organisation – and the measures for physical protection and protection against unauthorised access are useless.
- The only real hope of detecting this form of criminal activity is to set up adequate procedures for auditing the systems.

Privacy and data protection

Try to remember the title – the date is of least importance.

The UK Data Protection Act (1984), became part of business law three years later after firms had been given time to comply with its provisions.

It affects every commercial, business and government organisation that uses computers.

- The aim of the Act is to provide certain rights of access for citizens to any data of a personal nature which concerns that individual and is held in computerised form.
- The Act will be replaced in October 1998 and will cover certain paper-based as well as computer records. For major principles see page 94.

The Act requires that:

The eight principles – these deserve your attention!

- The information to be contained in personal data shall be obtained, and personal data shall be processed, fairly and lawfully.
- Personal data shall be held only for one or more specified and lawful purposes.
- Personal data held for any purpose or purposes shall not be used or disclosed in any manner incompatible with that purpose or those purposes.
- Personal data held for any purpose or purposes shall be adequate, relevant and not excessive in relation to that purpose or those purposes.

- Personal data shall be accurate and, where necessary, kept up to date.
- Personal data held for any purpose or purposes shall not be kept for longer than is necessary for the purpose or those purposes.
- An individual shall be entitled:
  at reasonable intervals and without undue time or expense

  (i) to be informed by any data user whether he holds personal data of which that individual is the subject; and
  (ii) to access any such data held by a data user; and

  where it is appropriate, to have such data corrected or erased.
- Appropriate security measures shall be taken against unauthorised access to, or alteration, disclosure or destruction of, personal data and against accidental loss or destruction of personal data.

Personal data is defined, for the purposes of the Act:

as data relating to living individuals who can be identified from that data alone or from its amalgamation with other data held by the user.

The Act specifies the following three elements involved:

1. the **data user** (the individual or organisation that has collected and computerised the data)
2. any **personal data** relating to **other individuals**
3. the **data subject** (the individual to whom the data refers).

The Act gives the data subject the right to:

- request from the data user copies of any record relating to the data subject
- to request that should any of the records prove incorrect or inaccurate they be corrected.

If the data user does not comply, the data subject has recourse to the Data Protection Registrar, any tribunal or the Courts.

The Data Protection Registrar:

- is responsible for the register
- promotes observance of the Act
- advises on matters relating to it
- investigates any complaints emanating from data subjects.

There are a number of principles to the Act and several categories of exemption from its provisions. In particular, one of the principles is that:

'Appropriate security measures shall be taken against unauthorised access to, or alteration, disclosure or destruction of, personal data and against accidental loss or destruction of personal data.'

- As far as is known, there have been no major claims against data users for breach of the Act, but it is essential that all organisations comply with its requirements.
- Part of the IS/IT strategy must be to ensure that the provisions of the Act are recognised.
- One person (the compliance officer) in the organisation should be responsible for all matters relating to the Act including ensuring that all the necessary registrations are made.

Learn the basic details of the Act.

EU directive on data protection

To aid and regulate the flow of data across national boundaries and to promote the single European market, in October 1995 The Council of Ministers adopted the European Directive on the protection of individuals with regard to the processing of personal data and on the free movement of such data.

- Member States are obliged to implement the provisions of the Directive within a three-year period.
- The Directive applies whenever personal data is processed wholly or partly by automatic means and also to certain forms of manual systems.
- Processing of personal data will be legitimate only in specified situations, where 'the data subject has unambiguously given his consent'.
- The data subject must be given details of the data holder's name and address and must also be informed of the parties to whom the data may be disclosed and of the existence of a right of access.

Exceptions to this provision may be made where the **requirement to inform** the subject would prejudice the maintenance of public order or what is described as the 'supervision and verification functions of a public authority'.

The subject need not be informed where this would be impossible, would involve a 'disproportionate effort' or would run 'counter to the overriding legitimate interests of the controller or similar interests of a third party'.

The Directive adopts a broad definition of the term '**sensitive data**' as encompassing indications as to 'racial or ethnic origin, political opinions, religious or philosophical beliefs, trade union membership, and ... health or sex life'. Such data may only be processed with 'explicit consent' of the data subject'.

The right of a data subject to obtain access to data held concerning them – and to change any errors – is one important element of a data protection law. The Directive's proposals are broadly in line with those currently operating in the United Kingdom.

A number of significant differences may be noted:

- There is no provision for refusal of access to medical data as is presently the case under the Data Protection Act (1984).

- Where access may be denied under specified exemptions the Directive provides that 'the supervisory authority shall be empowered to carry out the necessary checks, at the data subject's request, so as to verify the lawfulness of the processing'.

- If implemented, the Data Protection Registrar will have the power to inspect the data processing activities of national security agencies, a sector which is at present excluded totally from supervision.

Data and the media

There are **conflicts** between the **principle of data protection** and that of **freedom of expression**, which is integral to media activities.

Fundamental aspects of data protection such as subject access and the right to correct false information present a difficulty, especially where electronic databases contain the contents of previous issues of newspapers or periodicals.

The concept of **subject access** has also been identified as posing problems for the work of investigative journalists.

Supervisory agencies and notification

An independent supervisory agency has become part of data protection legislation within Europe. A number of powers and duties are to be part of the role of a supervisory agency:

- to investigate subject's complaints relating to exemptions from the Directive, such as those concerned with national security

- to order the cessation of data processing
- to order the blocking, erasure or rectification of data
- to bring complaints regarding processing to the attention of the legal authorities.

The supervisory authority must be consulted when any administrative measures or regulations concerned with data protection are being drawn up.

Questions

Core topic 18 Security, the Data Protection Act and EU Directives

1 Name the four major areas of information systems (IS) security.

2 Why is it important for a company to protect its data from unauthorised access?

3 What are the major provisions of the Data Protection Act 1984? Why was the Act passed by parliament?

4 If you were to devise an IS security policy for your company, what would you put in your proposals and why?

5 What steps should a company take to ensure the physical safety of any data it might hold? What might be the consequences for a company if data is lost or destroyed?

Extension topic 23

Legal aspects

The driving force on security is the Data Protection Act.

The need for a corporate information technology security policy and its role within an organisation

If an organisation sets up an information systems strategy, then one of the concerns should be the security of the resulting system and the data and information stored.

- Remember that the organisation has probably spent a lot of time and money in assembling the equipment and the data. It should be protected!
- Also bear in mind that the organisation probably holds details about customers and suppliers and it has obligations to them under the Data Protection Act.

Security is therefore concerned with protection and can be divided into the following areas:

- protection against loss or damage to equipment – to include:
  - hardware – file servers, workstations, bridges, links, cables and the like
  - software – program code and resulting files
- protection against loss of data – to include:
  - unauthorised amendment of files
  - unauthorised copying of program code and data files
  - unauthorised viewing of data files.

Note this division carefully – think logically.

The security strategy needs to look at the system as a whole –

- the physical links (the infrastructure), and then at
- various individual systems, for example stock control, financial administration and production.

Security strategy is not a static process – 'once written never to be reviewed!' – it must be constantly reviewed along with other aspects of the business. It is very easy to forget operational developments.

For example: site engineers get issued with laptop computers containing data, maps and diagrams of customers' premises –

- Have security procedures been written to cope with these new machines?
- Do these machines have security software and codes equal to that of the main system?

Your security is only as good as the weakest link.

Many of the crimes and abuses of computer systems take place from within an organisation.

There is probably no foolproof way of preventing such actions. However, the security strategy needs to build in regular and systematic checks.

- A big deterrent is the likelihood of being caught. If staff know that checks are made, they are less likely to chance a criminal act.
- Awareness of security policy is an important aspect of working with information systems.
- If, at all levels of the business, security is seen as important and is built into the company training programme, then it is likely to succeed.

- Staff need to see that breaches of security are treated seriously, possibly leading to dismissal.

Awareness could also be raised by **involving the staff** in working for **accreditation to a national security standard such as BS7799**, the principles of which are shown below:

- development of a security policy
- the organisation of security
- classification and control of company assets
- security of all employees
- security of company premises
- management of computers and networks
- control of access to systems
- systems development and maintenance
- business continuity planning
- compliance with the law such as the Data Protection Act.

Staff could also be involved in professional training such as that accredited by the British Computer Society.

Extension topic 23 Legal aspects

1. Why should a company adopt a security strategy to protect both IT equipment and data?

2. What are the main problems to be taken into account when establishing a company IT security strategy?

3. Why do you think companies are so reluctant to discuss their security problems and to prosecute those of their employees who breach security?

Core Topic 19: IT and the professional

Codes of practice

A code of practice is **not a legal document**, just a **declaration of intent**. Bodies such as BT have codes of practice which may go beyond current legislation because:

- legislation is lagging behind fast moving technology, e.g. surveillance cameras
- the company wants to promote a **quality image** above and beyond legal requirements to boost customer confidence.

Many IT companies have introduced codes of practice for both the above reasons. This has been encouraged by lead bodies such as the British Computer Society as it also hopes to improve standards and professionalism within the IT industry.

Industry structure model

Standards for training and development.

The BCS has produced a comprehensive set of standards for the training and development of all those working in information systems and related fields.

- This is called the industry structure model (ISM) and it defines over 200 different **functions** in information systems – including programmers, software engineers, network specialists and hybrid managers – at ten levels of **responsibility** and **technical expertise**.
- The ISM is used extensively in the UK and overseas as a means of planning training and measuring its effectiveness against an independent, industry-accepted benchmark.
- It is also used to help plan career development and as a reference point for an individual's level of responsibility.
- The ISM is regularly reviewed to ensure it is reflecting the changing nature of the IT industry.

Specifically, it is used to:

- compose customised job descriptions from standardised roles/tasks
- assess the competence of IS
- establish individual and corporate training and development needs
- provide training to recognised standards
- plot career development paths
- establish staffing and recruitment needs
- identify skills shortages.

Roles rather than jobs

Information systems jobs often involve several different roles. For this reason, ISM is structured as a simple matrix of over 200 roles, categorised by ten levels of responsibility and competence.

- The **tasks** performed within each role are clearly stated, along with the **experience and skills** required, and training and development targets.
- Details are given of all relevant vocational and professional **qualifications**, including Scottish/National Vocational Qualifications (S/NVQs).

Nine functional areas are covered:

- management
- support and administration
- policy and planning
- systems development and maintenance
- service delivery
- technical advice and consultancy
- customer relations
- education and training
- quality.

The IT professional should be well qualified and also have good interpersonal skills (the ability to get on with and motivate people).

Questions

Core topic 19 IT and the professional

1. As a junior employee in an IT company, you wish to know possible promotion and career paths. How can the industry structure model help you in this?

2. A company is trying to gain a quality award and has been advised to introduce a 'code of practice'. Explain why this is.

3. Why might a customer use a company with a code of practice rather than one without?

4. Outline the industry structure model and give reasons why it was developed.

5. What qualities would you expect from an IT professional?

6. How could the ISM help in setting the salary for a newly developed post such as an Internet librarian?

Extension topic 24: Training

The need for training is an important part of making employees feel comfortable with IT.

- If a company is going to survive it must have up-to-date information systems which are understood by all the staff.
- The company needs to set out a training strategy.

Methods to aid staff training might include:

- computer-based training
- interactive video instruction
- on-line tutorials
- step through guides
- formal training courses.

Effective training is part of software success.

People have high expectations of computers and multimedia—from their experiences with PCs and television. If you do not live up to these expectations, your credibility will be hurt.

Computer-based training

- Trainee able to work at own pace.
- Allows for graduated lessons, progress monitoring, and feedback.
- Can be used in tutor-led classes or as part of a distance learning package.

Interactive video instruction

- Generally a training course based on video shots of the operations to be carried out.
- Video gives an overview of the tasks followed by 'lessons' with required target output.

On-line tutorials

- These can be part of the package sold with the software and make up part of the 'help files', for example: help files within Microsoft Office or Perfect Office (Corel) or Lotus Smartsuite/Smart Office.
- These files can be accessed at any time during the running of the software. Thus they are 'on-line' – 'live' – 'in real time'.

Step through guides

- These take the trainee on a 'step-by-step' guide through the major facilities within the selected software.
- Many texts have been published on how to use major pieces of software such as: Microsoft Word and Excel, Lotus Notes and Smartsuite.
- These can have exercises or small tasks built in to each step in order to assist understanding of the software.

Questions

Extension topic 24 Training

1. In what circumstances would an interactive video training system be appropriate?

2. Why is it important for a company to develop a training strategy as far as information technology/systems is concerned?

3. Outline an appropriate strategy to introduce operations staff to a new word-processing system.

4. Outline a case to senior management to convince them a new training system using interactive video to replace current step through texts is worth adopting.

Extension topic 25

User support

The range and sophistication of software has developed rapidly over the last five years. The power of computers to exploit the facilities within the software has also grown.

Not everyone is an information technology expert, not even those who work for companies who have a strong commitment to the use of technology in their businesses.

Thus in order to get the best from software, and to ensure repeat business, software manufacturers have produced a range of user support.

These include:

- printed manuals
- on-line help pages and demos within the software supplied
- telephone helplines
- on-line bulletin boards
- Internet pages with e-mail addresses.

Note that a range of support does exist.

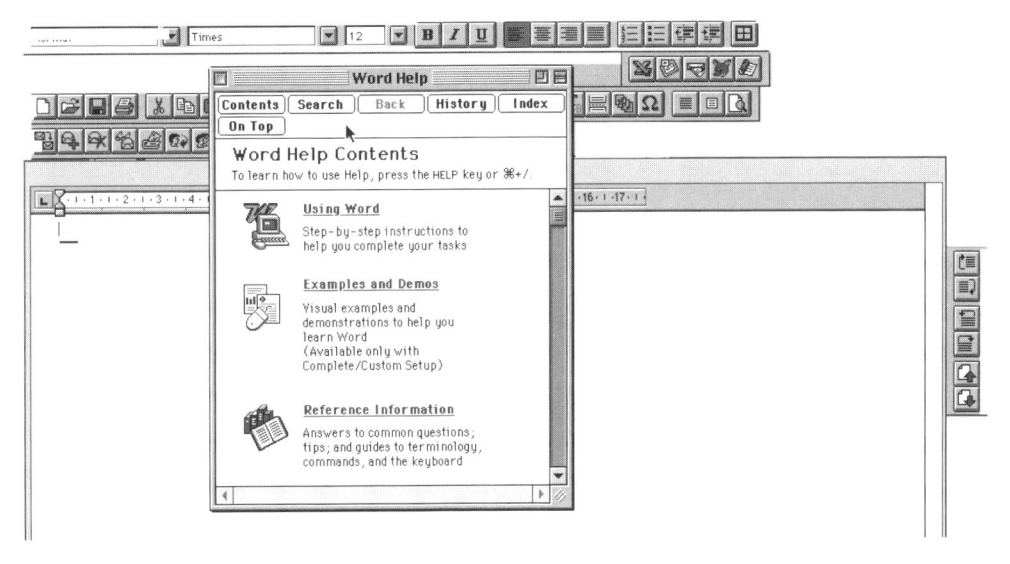

Figure 30

Clearly the amount of support that a company can provide must be related to the expected income from the sales of the software.

- A modestly priced piece of software does not necessarily mean that the manufacturer is unwilling to support it, because it could have world-wide volume sales.

- An expensive piece of software might not have wide appeal, therefore a manufacturer might not be able to offer a great deal of technical support without compromising profitability.

If 'industry standard packages' are being used such as Microsoft Word, Lotus Smart Office or Quark Express then support for these products could be extended by reference to:

- an existing user base
- support articles in the computer press
- utilities by third-party manufacturers
- specialist bulletin boards
- Internet pages
- user forums.

USER SUPPORT 103

Case study: Brannigan, Lewis

Brannigan, Lewis are a large firm of solicitors in Deansgate, Manchester. They employ five solicitors and ten clerical and support staff. They have recently introduced a new computer network with links via the Internet to legal databases as well as sharing client data within the practice. They have a very heavy word-processing need, preparing case briefs and other client documentation.

They need to have support for their staff in use of the Internet, e-mailing and word-processing. They need to provide special help for new members of staff.

Think about how you would answer this question.

Select and justify an appropriate type of user support for Brannigan, Lewis.

Users come to systems with various levels of competence:

- expert users
- frequent users
- occasional users.

Reasons for choice are important at A level. Get beyond description!

Different levels of competence require different kinds of support.

- Expert users might need little help to complete tasks.
- Frequent users will need some guidance and reminders about how to proceed.
- Occasional users may find it difficult to get going and there will need to be some familiarisation with the system in order to restore both confidence and competence.

Don't take users for granted. All might need support.

Questions

Extension topic 25 User support

1 List the range of help and support facilities available to IT users.

2 Why has the range of support facilities increased and improved in recent years?

3 If you were to design an on-line help facility for users, what six major elements would you include in your facility to help:

   novice users?
   occasional users?
   expert users?

   Justify each entry in your list.

4 Research tends to show that users are very reluctant to read manuals to help them understand a computer or applications package. How can you explain this reluctance? What could software designers do to help overcome this problem?

Extension topic 26

Project management and effective IT teams

Tendency to produce 'woolly' answers here. Note the bulleted points.

Many of the developments within IT systems call for substantial changes to existing practices and technology. These changes are likely to be beyond the scope of one person. A more effective approach would be to bring in specialist help in order to look at all aspects of the problem.

The success of the team will be dependent upon a careful definition of the problem.

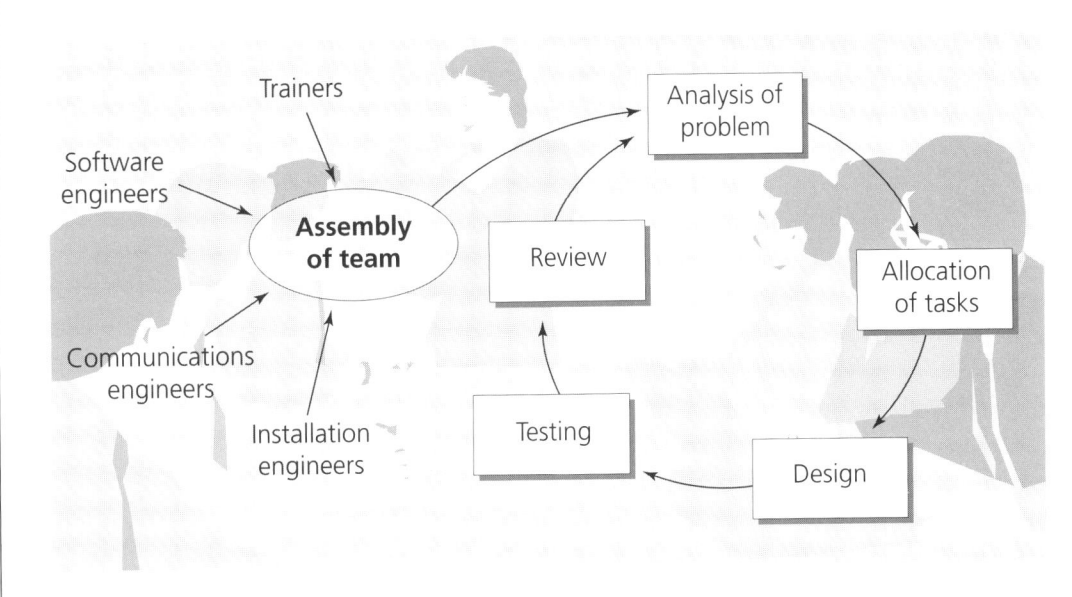

Figure 31

A good team will need:

- sound leadership
- an appropriate allocation of tasks
- an adherence to defined standards
- sensible budgeting
- control of costs
- monitoring progress
- ability to deliver results on time.

Facilities management

When deciding whether to maintain an in-house IS/IT department or to put it out to facilities management, there are a number of considerations:

- What is the total cost of recruiting and employing internal staff?
  It is not simply the salary. There will be recruitment costs, typically 20% of the employee's salary, employer's national insurance, training and any fringe benefits such as car, life assurance, pension scheme, free medical insurance, etc.
- Could new/additional skills be provided more cheaply by an outside company?
- Are the skills required 100% of the time or only on an occasional basis?
- What are the main considerations for the business?
- Is cost reduction or flexibility the highest priority?

PROJECT MANAGEMENT AND EFFECTIVE IT TEAMS 105

Facilities management (FM) is a service whereby a company undertakes to run the client's information technology systems for a given period.

> *This is a specialist definition and needs learning to gain full marks.*

Benefits

There are some benefits to using FM from the company's (that is, the client's) viewpoint.

- It is possible to determine exactly the **level of expenditure** for IS/IT service. The FM company has to provide the agreed level of service for the agreed price; if the service costs more than was expected, the FM company has to bear the cost.

- If there is a need for occasional use of very specialised staff or equipment, the FM company can **spread these scarce resources** over a number of sites and **gain economies of scale**. This strategy would be part of a move towards the 'flexible firm' where as much of the non-operational and support work as possible is subcontracted.

- It is often difficult to make internal IS departments set up service level agreements with their client base. Using facilities management contracts is often an effective way of achieving a **known, defined level of service**.

Disadvantages

- A service level agreement might say that 'All fault calls will be logged and responded to within 30 minutes'. This could be rather misleading . A 'response' might simply be a telephone call to say that nothing can be done for several days. A fixed time is what is really required.

- In times of crisis, when dealing with an internal department, it is possible to 'tear up the rule book' to get an urgent problem resolved. An FM contract would not necessarily provide for this level of flexibility.

- If, in moving to FM, the client company has had to make many of its existing IS staff redundant, then the cost of re-establishing the IS/IT department would be considerable if the client had a rethink about its position or the facilities manager went out of business.

Core Topic 20: Role of IT and its social impact

The topic of the social impact of IT is very large and so only a few ideas are given here for revision. You would be advised to read about the subject.

An opportunity to collect/use real examples.

- Look for articles in **newspapers** and **magazines** as well as text **books**.
- Great resources can also be found on the **Internet**.
- Learning a **case study** that includes many of the topics below is also a good idea.

The themes likely to be found in questions include:

- **dependence** on IT systems
- what would happen if they **failed**?
- IT bringing about **change**
- **employment**
- **benefits** and **drawbacks** of using IT.

Impact on individuals

Leisure games

Large increase in the use of computer games. Problems include:

- wasting time
- no social interaction
- addiction, young children playing violent games
- repetitive strain injury (RSI).

Advantages:
- can be relaxing
- some of the problem-solving type have educational benefit
- 'games' can be included in teaching software
- no real problems if it fails.

Education

- More use of the information learning technology approach ILT.
- Developed from computer-assisted instruction (repetitive learning) and computer-assisted learning.
- Computer tries to replace 'teacher'.
- This approach does not suit all learners.
- 'Computer fatigue'.
- Could be viewed as an attempt to reduce costs.
- Home education packages, e.g. Encarta very popular.
- Remote learning (rather than visit a college, a virtual college is set up using e-mail and conferencing).

Advantages:
- when can't attend school because of distance/weather (e.g. in Finland)
- able to work at own pace.

Disadvantages:
- isolating
- relies on equipment.

Household finances

Many people with PCs now look after their household budget.

Control

Many mechanisms such as TVs, video, etc. have **embedded systems**. Some modern houses have had networks and intelligent control of lights, burglar alarms, central heating etc. installed. Big impact if system fails.

Communication

With the advent of the Internet it is now possible to have long distance telephone calls cheaply.

Social

- As individuals we are becoming more **information aware** and will demand it more readily.
- The spread of IT makes for **less social contact**, e.g. telephone queuing systems and touch-tone banks.

Health

- We depend on the use of IT in many aspects of health care, from hospital appointments and record cards, to emergency monitoring systems in intensive care.
- The failure of such systems would be life-threatening in the worst case.
- Remote diagnostics (diagnostics using expert systems – a bit like a Radio doctor in the Australian outback).

Cashless society

- Pay is made into bank accounts automatically (**EFT** – electronic funds transfer).
- Cheques and plastic cards have replaced a lot of cash transactions.
- There have been experiments with Mondex **smart cards** to become even more cashless. However, cash point machines are being more used than ever.
- Advantages include speed and not having to carry cash.
- Disadvantages include possible fraud and what happens if system fails or card is lost.

Work related

- IT has made an improvement in many work environments.
- The electronic office has meant changes for many employees – see below.
- Some jobs have been **de-skilled**, e.g. the worker who now looks after a robot that sprays the cars that s/he once sprayed.
- Many individuals have had to undergo **re-training** due to the introduction of IT and the phrase '**life-long learning**' has been coined.
- Redundancies: although re-training is often offered to the individual, **redundancies** (sometimes voluntary, sometimes not) often occur when more efficient IT systems are introduced. There is some evidence that IT systems are **not as flexible** in some situations as human workers, and some **re-hiring** has occurred in some areas.

Health and safety

- The individual should be more aware of IT related health and safety issues such as repetitive strain injury (RSI), radiation hazard from the monitor and posture problems from sitting a long time in front of a VDU.

Work patterns: individuals' work patterns have been affected:

- IT has allowed the introduction of **flexi-time**, where workers can choose, within limits, when to work.
- The IT systems keep track of hours worked.
- The advent of the Internet and private WANs have allowed people to work from home (**home-working**).
- Advantages include no journey times, less pollution/stress, working in known environment, flexible hours, e.g. if single parent.
- Disadvantages include social isolation and possible disruption, e.g. noisy kids.
- There is a move to farm out IT work to workers in other countries, as their wage costs are lower.
- **Teleconferencing** is on the increase.
- Advantages: no wasted journeys/time, less pollution, cheaper than travelling around the country.
- Disadvantages include: difficult to have large conference, no eye-to-eye meetings, lack of concrete outcomes, e.g. signed contract.

Impact on organisations

Service sector

Organisations have seen a rapid increase in the use of IT to support **management decisions**, as well as in **day-to-day** operations.

- **Fewer staff** needed, e.g. bank clerks replaced by cash point ATMs (automatic teller machines).
- Many companies **highly reliant** on computers, business would fold as no alternative system if total crash, e.g. airlines.

Health organisations have increased their use of computers, especially monitoring equipment. Many have date functions, so the **Millennium problem**, when many computers and embedded microprocessors will not know the difference between 1900 and 2000, **may prove fatal**.

Education

Education has seen IT as a **key skill** and it is taught at all levels. There are cost implications for keeping up to date, and the main culprit for making it necessary to upgrade is the sales of **home computers**. These are fuelled more by fashion than needs, as **many home PCs are only used to a fraction of their capabilities**.

Police

The police use computers for day-to-day record keeping, but also have expert systems that search for patterns within crime data. Much quicker and more reliable than manual systems. They use the Police National Computer for things like car identity checks.

Government

The French government uses its national WAN **Minitel** when the population vote during referendums.

Shops

Larger stores use computers which link sales to ordering systems, so stock levels in the warehouse can be kept as low as possible. When computers fail, estimated bills are the only alternative. Some large nationals do not use computers at their check-outs at all, but train and pay the check-out staff well.

Manufacturing sector

- Process control
- Robotics

The manufacturing sector uses computers in many stages, from research to design (**Computer-Assisted Design/Drafting**), to the use of computers in controlling the production process. Again a large reliance is put on the use of computers, and the old way of making products without the aid of computers will be largely forgotten.

Impact on society

Some of the points that could be discussed about the use of IT in society might include:

- Divisiveness: some people have computers and are computer literate, some cannot afford it.
- Less time/more stress: the pace of life increases as IT systems work faster, e.g. replies to e-mails demanded more quickly than letters.
- Computer crime: there has been an increase in computer crime – see section on computer misuse for details (page 91).
- Privacy: as more data is held about individuals it is becoming more difficult to police, so you might not be aware of what information is being held about you, or by whom.
- Disabilities: the use of computers has greatly enhanced the quality of life for many disabled people, e.g. Stephen Hawking.
- Global market: there is now considered to be a global market, but a problem has arisen when buying goods over the Internet – how does the taxman get his cut?

Questions

Core topic 20 Role of IT and its social impact

1 Individuals and organisations have become so dependent upon IT systems that the consequences of their failure could be catastrophic to the individual or the organisation.
   Give two different examples of types of IT system for which failure would be catastrophic. In each case explain why the failure could prove to be catastrophic.

2 A multi-national company is considering the use of 'teleconferencing'.

   a) What is meant by the term 'teleconferencing'?
   b) List the minimum facilities required to enable 'teleconferencing' to take place.
   c) Discuss two advantages and two disadvantages to the firm of using 'teleconferencing' as compared to traditional methods.

3 'Networked computer systems (e.g. Internet) will revolutionise the way in which we shop.' With the aid of specific examples, discuss this statement. Include in your discussion:
- The types of organisation likely to advertise on such systems.
- The capabilities and limitations of such systems for this activity.
- The potential security risks for the customers in using such systems.
- The organisational impact of such systems.
- The social impact of such systems.

Answers

Core topic 1 Nature and types of software

1. Memory management – making sure programs are located correctly in memory without overlapping or corruption; backing store management including looking after directory structure; controlling/communication with peripherals, e.g. sending data to printer.

2. Could be any utility program, e.g. file manager, which allows a disc to be formatted and files to be copied from hard to floppy.

3. More emphasis placed on involvement of the user as prototyping possible due to quick development times. Faster to develop solution but final solution might be slower to run as it is developed from a general purpose package rather than specialised solution.

4. Availability – takes time to develop specialised solution; reliability – off-the-shelf have large user base and support; cost – off-the-shelf can have economies of scale; features – off-the-shelf might have too many or too few features, bespoke fits exactly. Off-the-shelf less flexible in the long run.

5. Hardware is the physical equipment, e.g. a printer, a disc drive. Software is the programs required to control or use the hardware, e.g. operating systems or applications.

6. Payroll, stock control, invoicing.

7. File transfer – files may be moved easily between modules rather than have to export/import.

    Speed of use – switching between the modules does not mean closing and restarting the programs.

8. See Figure 2, page 6. The user communicates with the application, which communicates with the operating system, which communicates with the hardware.

9. Tailoring is the process of using a generic package to provide a solution to a problem, by customising the generic package. It can involve the use of programming techniques as well as the application building features of the package. Examples might be an automated mailmerge database for a club, including templates and record selection features, created using a word-processor. The advantage in a business situation is that the package would be available and the solution can be tailored to fit the business exactly.

Core topic 2 Peripherals

1. A "concept keyboard" where the regions of the keyboard can be programmed and an overlay used, e.g. pub till, junior school computer.

2. Where it is not desirable to use a keyboard, e.g. tourist office public enquiry system.

3. A bar code scanner uses reflected laser light to determine the pattern of lines and spaces in a bar code, e.g. library ticket. An OMR (optical mark reader) uses reflected light to determine the presence or absence of marks, e.g. multiple choice exam papers. An OCR (optical character reader) uses the patterns of reflected light to determine the printed text.

4. Disagree because: sound interfaces are difficult to use in noisy environments; sound interfaces cannot be used by some disabled groups, e.g. deaf; keyboards are a cheap alternative to the memory and processor power needed for speech interfaces; speech interfaces are not 100% accurate.

5. Optical mark reader, national lottery tickets; magnetic ink character recognition, used on bank cheques to hold account number and sort code; optical character reader, used to read special fonts, some tills use this.

6. (a) colour ink jet, cheap to buy, OK for low volume printing, good photo quality available; (b) dot matrix, cheap to buy and run, reliable, carbon copy possible; (c) laser jet, cheaper

to use with large volume than ink jet, colour not needed, more expensive to buy; (d) Fast laser as very large volumes of bills, possibly chain line impact printer for carbon copies.

7 Magnetic swipe card holds only a few 10s of bytes compared to 600Mbyte; magnetic tape, serial access only, holds more than CD, better for large volume back-ups; magnetic disc holds more than 2Gbyte, access times faster as more heads per surface.

8 Multi-pen plotter. The paper is held by suction or electrostatic charge on a flat bed. The colour pens move in small steps vertically and horizontally to create the image.

9 They are cheap and readily available, easily transportable and useable as most computers have a floppy drive.

Extension topic 1 Bitmaps and OCR

1 The picture is made up of pixels, each pixel is controlled by a part of memory. If black and white, each part of memory only needs to be 1 bit (1/8 byte). If it was scanned in 256 colours then each pixel would require 1 byte, so the file would be eight times larger.

Core topic 3 User interfaces/terminology

1 (a) Use of coloured icons and sound output to help stimulate learning, touch screen input. (b) Mouse pen or graphics tablet, large screen with high resolution. Shortcut menus and macros. (c) Command line interface with control commands for Turtle. Macros and programming elements, i.e. sequence selection and repetition.

2 Speed once commands are learnt, difficult to learn commands. (Harder for a first time user, easier for expert.) More flexible, not all commands might be available in the menu system.

3 The ability to record and name a sequence of keystrokes or commands, and play them back using the name only as a command.

4 Hands-free operation, some commands have to be learnt, difficult to use if quiet required, or in noisy environment. No use to deaf/dumb but good for sight impaired users.

5 A menu, or navigation tree, shows the route through a WIMP interface system and how the various forms and buttons are connected.

6 A dialogue box is a form that gives the user options. The user makes choices, using text boxes, option buttons and drop down lists. An example is the Print dialogue box which allows the user to choose which printer, the pages or selection required and the number of copies.

7 The help and/or tutorial would be used by the new user in order to familiarise themselves with the features of the software. Shortcut keys and macros would be used in preference to mouse clicks by the experienced user in order to save time.

Extension topic 2 Human–computer interface

1 Screen buttons of adequate size; commonly used ones nearer the centre of screen; shape of mouse to suit hand without tiring; similarly keyboard to reduce strain. Shortcuts for experienced users.

2 The user has to form requests using a restricted vocabulary and grammar, but the resulting sentences are English-like in construction, e.g. "Show sales figures for all salesmen for July as pie chart."

3 Families of software share similar features, so the new user only has to learn one package and can then transfer the skills learned more easily to the others. Menus and buttons would be in similar positions and even the main menu bar could be almost identical.

Core topic 4 Networks and distributed systems

1 Advantages: sharing of resources such as printers and disc drives; sharing of data and software; communication between computers.

Disadvantages: possibility of a system failure bringing down whole system rather than one machine; viruses more easily spread.

2. Move operating systems/applications to local machines so network traffic reduced. Sufficient RAM for caching files on server, so frequently used files are read from RAM rather than disc. Employ a bridge to segment the network and put a server on each side of the bridge to have the network traffic in each section, but still allow access to shared resources, e.g. printers.

3. An Intranet is a local area network resource using a browser system to open and link documents and is owned and controlled locally. The Internet is a wide area network outside a company accessed via a modem and browser software.

4. See figures 8, 9 and 10 (page 19).

5. The sharing of data and information across the sites makes for quicker management information. Communication across the sites using e-mail is quicker and cheaper when there are multiple recipients. Video conferencing cuts down on transport and accommodation costs.

6. LAN speeds are of the order of 500Kbytes per second data transfer, WANs range from 900bytes p.s. to 11Kbytes per second, i.e. 50–500 times slower.

Extension topic 3 Repeaters, bridges and backbones

1. A repeater is a device that regenerates a digital signal that has been degraded by its transmission. A hub is a device that is used in a star network to link the traffic coming from the various limbs of the star. A bridge is used to segment a network (then put a server on each side of the bridge to halve the network traffic in each segment), but still allow access to shared resources, e.g. printers from one side of the bridge to the other.

Extension topic 4 The OSI model

1. The OSI model is the Open System Interconnection model that describes a layered set of protocols and the rules for the input and output to each layer. It solves the complex problem of describing network communications and allows networks of different types to be interconnected if the protocols follow the rules. It also allows hardware to be manufactured by different companies, again if they follow the rules.

Extension topic 5 Distribution

1. Distributed systems can mean not only the distribution of processing power in the form of networks as opposed to centralised mainframe installations, but also the possibility of distributing the data and the control over that data, using a network.

Core topic 5 Role of communication systems

1. If person not reachable via phone, e-mail messages could be left and the sender could be notified when they are read.

2. e-mail costs less over long distance than telephone or fax, can have multiple recipients, can include files as well as text. Faxes good for hand-written documents as e-mail can only attach a scanned document so fax quicker. Telephone good for personal touch and two-way conversation.

3. The advent of browsers with search engines has allowed users to search keyword indexes for matches and to be able to download and process associated information from remote sites across the globe.

4. e-mail allows the same message to be sent to multiple recipients at the same time, thus saving costs. It also allows simple forwarding and reply and also the proof of opening of e-mail. The speed of response is quicker if the e-mail is checked regularly.

5. Simplex – one direction only, e.g. TV. Half-duplex, both directions but not at the same time, e.g. two-way radio. Duplex, both directions at the same time, e.g. telephone.

Extension topic 6 Packet switching systems

1. A packet contains the sender's address, the recipient's address, the data, the packet number and error correction data. It is more secure than a circuit link as the packets can take different routes. If an error occurs, only the affected packets need to be re-transmitted rather than the whole message.

2. No time wasted establishing link to other computers. More secure as packets can go different routes. Cheaper when long distance, packet local charge only. Errors more quickly corrected as affected packets re-transmitted, not whole message.

3. Packets are dynamically routed by the nodes in the PSS and it's possible for the packets to arrive out of sequence.

Core topic 6 Portability of data

1. School computer uses different operating system, e.g. Macintosh/PC; software at school different, e.g. Word and AmiPro, and filters not installed in one or other; software at home later version than school's.

2. A *de facto* standard grows from a popular piece of software that is widely used. A formal standard is agreed by a number of companies/organisations.

3. An export filter allows you to "save as" your files into a number of possible formats, some standard such as RTF or ASCII, some *de facto* e.g. Word. An import filter allows you to import data in different formats from the one used by the package you are using.

4. Different computer manufacturers were using different binary codes for the same letter of the alphabet, so when interconnection was required, a translator program had to be used. This became unwieldy, so a common format was agreed.

5. To think very carefully before opting for such a package. The company needs to consider growth of the system and the necessity at some stage to read other data sources and to save in other formats. However, in the meantime they need to use a package which will convert files to a format which can be read by the new database package. An application such as Excel has excellent file conversion facilities which include CSV, Dbase, DIF (Data Interchange Format) and Lotus 1-2-3.

6. The company must ensure that the data it already holds can be backed up into a format which can be read by applications supported by the new operating system. For example, all text-based files to be backed up into TEXT format or ASCII (American Standard Code for Information Interchange) format or spreadsheet tables backed up into CSV (Comma Separated Variable) format.

7. Check out the software in school. Make sure that this software is able to read TEXT files. Work on your files both at home and in school in TEXT format only until you are satisfied that all the necessary information has been gathered and ordered into the file. Decide where the final edited version is going to be produced – at home or in school. Read the TEXT file into your chosen application. Edit to taste – bold, underline, etc. – and save the file in its new format, for example, WORD.DOC or RTF, then print.

Core topic 7 Security of data

1. (a) Twice daily back-up of files to DAT tape, removed off site at night. (b) Transaction log of all changes and daily archive of main files. (c) Back-up of files to floppy after each session. (d) Daily back-up of files to floppy removed off site. (e) Mirror system, all transactions duplicated. Nightly back-up of files, copies kept off site.

2. User accounts and passwords, with file access restricted by supervisor, to stop unauthorised access. Virus detection software installed on server and work stations to trap virus corruption.

3. An audit trail is a log of events concerning a resource such as a data file. It records what action was attempted, at what time, by whom, and what the outcome was. If a file has been illegally accessed, the trail can show when and by whom.

4 Data encryption is the process of converting data in plain text into cyphercode. The two most common methods are substitution and transposition. Once encrypted, the data becomes unintelligible, until it is decrypted.

5 People not changing default passwords; observation of password entry; using a common password, e.g. letmein; writing down passwords.

6 A computer virus is a piece of code hidden in a file. It may be harmless, but more usually attacks a computer's memory or hard disc and causes corruption and loss of data. It also copies itself onto other files, thus infecting other files and possibly other machines if the files are transferred and then used. Protection is by virus protection software that recognises the pattern of the code from a database of virus types, and also warns when attempts are made to access sensitive areas of the hard disc or memory.

Core topic 8 Software capabilities

1 Company must draw up a list of requirements which may also include current software standards of the site. Research done into possible software – using software reviews, evaluation copies of software. Cost benefit analysis undertaken.

2 Searching using OR and AND functions, and combinations of them. Being able to add fields without incurring data loss.

3 Prototyping is the process of building models to show to users; they can be non-working, pilot or developmental. User makes suggested improvements. Has increased as fourth generation languages allow quick development of applications.

4 With embedding, a snapshot of the data is used, whereas linking links to the file giving the latest version. If file is updated, snapshot is not, linked view is.

5 A benchmark is a term used to describe a standard test with predicted outcomes, the results of which can be used to compare the performance of different products, e.g. a benchmark time to re-paginate a 100-page document.

Extension topic 7 Software to support specialist applications

Ways of providing a solution:

user written/internal development team or department/external software house to examination board specification. Use of generic package(s) customised to meet specific needs of the examination board. Specific, i. e. purchased from a company that specialises in software for examination boards.

Issues that should be considered before solution is selected:

Cost of alternative solutions – for generic, large numbers sold so prices are low, less so with alternatives.

Development and testing time for alternative solutions – generic is thoroughly tested, reducing time. Not so for alternatives.

Ease of use of alternative approaches.

Extensive user base of generic suggests better user interface.

Quality/reliability/existence of documentation provided – generic provided with extensive documentation, others may not be.

Appropriateness of solution – generic may need considerable work in customising to suit specific requirements.

Configurability – generic may require in-depth knowledge of the package to configure the application. Bespoke should already match requirements.

Upgrade paths provided by alternative approaches – new versions of product, dependence on small company.

User support overheads incurred by alternative solutions – wide user base/size of supplier organisation and ability to cope with support overheads.

Compatibility of alternatives with existing hardware base – need for upgrades, additional memory, faster processors, etc.

Compatibility with existing software – transferability of existing data files, interface with other generic packages, etc.

How do alternatives relate to corporate strategies for hardware/software licensing/purchase?

Core topic 9 Upgradability

1. Ability to port current data to new system. Reliability of new system.

   Does new software meet existing company software standards? Level of support available. Features available cover all proposed use. Ability to link to other software currently used by company. Cost of retraining staff. Need to upgrade hardware. Compatibility with current operating system. Availability of new software – is one available sooner than other?

2. Possible hardware upgrade to memory or processor. Staff retraining in the use of the new software.

3. Backward compatibility, i.e. the ability to use data files created in earlier versions in the new system. Technical support for the old and new versions.

Core topic 10 Reliability of software

1. This depends on what is meant by reliable. Does it always load up? Does it always give consistent results? Much of this depends on the machine on which the software is being used, where the software is being used, the number of times the software is used (occasionally errors occur), whether a back-up copy of the original software has been retained. User error – where the incorrect data items have been entered. Programmer omission – in a complex program, maybe not all cases of use have been identified and the program raises an error message or just stops!

   Once software has been released, it's down to the user to maintain reliability by using the product sensibly. Not everyone does!

2. Solving a problem using formal methods and a formal language such as ADA is a mathematical procedure where the problem is described in terms of a mathematical expression, and the expression is solved. This solution is written in the formal language so that the code is correct at the first attempt (assuming the initial description is logically correct!)

3. If it waits until all the errors are fixed then the market may be lost to competitors. It may be involved in testing the software using beta copies. It may be such a complex piece of software that it is not possible to simulate all possible conditions.

4. In functional testing, the system is treated as a black box and the inputs and expected outcomes are matched against actual outcomes. No internal working of the system is considered. In logical testing, all routes and combinations through the system are tested.

5. Software may be tested by a large beta user base, e.g. Windows 97. Software may endanger life if not working properly, e.g. space shuttle control system.

6. Testing takes time and with modern complex software there is not enough time to thoroughly test every conceivable combination of circumstances before a product is launched. To find all the bugs might mean losing out to a competitor.

Core topic 11 Configurability of hard/software

1. A driver program is a piece of software designed to interface a peripheral, e.g. a video card. Without them many or all of the features of the peripheral will not be available.

2. Many or all of the features of the peripheral will not be available. The operation of the printer will be unpredictable and may even be damaged.

3. Instead of setting jumpers and dip switches to make choices, these are kept in electrically alterable read only memory and can be changed by configuration software, or by the operating system itself ("plug and play").

4 Incorrect drivers can affect the performance of peripherals, e.g. incorrect hard disc driver. Settings for things such as cache memory are kept in EAROM (electrically alterable read only memory) and can affect the performance. Set-up software can check and alter these settings.

5 Early systems required hardware settings to be altered using jumpers or dip switches and meant extensive reading of manual and sometimes dismantling of equipment to reach these switches.

6 Physical switches used to make choices on the set-up of hardware. More modern components have the setting held in electrically alterable read only memory (EAROM) on the device, and it is changed either by set-up software, or directly by a plug and play operating system.

Core topic 12 Modes of processing

1 The speed at which the output is required after the processing. The need for dialogue or interaction between the user and the application.

2 Textual data can be searched, split and joined but no arithmetic can be performed on it. Sound data can be processed to produce effects, e.g. delay, echo, reversal, editing out noise. Image data can be processed to change colours, e.g. drawing package. Numeric data can have arithmetic operations performed on it.

3 The output is available quickly enough after the processing to affect the input, e.g. real-time control of a missile: the input might be speed and direction, processed to produce information that says the missile is banking, the output used to adjust the input to correct it.

4 The data arrives and is collected in batches, e.g. mail orders each morning by post. The output is not required immediately, there can be a delay between processing and output. There is no need for interaction between the user and the application while the process is running. The hit rate of the file is high.

5 This is where the user is on line to the computer and the transaction might be processed immediately, or may be stored for later batch processing.

6 This is where the user is connected directly to the computer and the transaction is completed almost immediately. An example might be flight bookings; the speed is necessary to avoid double bookings.

7 (a) Batch, as the data arrives in batches and the output is not required immediately.
  (b) Real-time, as the output has to react to the input, e.g. to trim a dive.
  (c) On-line transaction processing to avoid double bookings.

8 The sound envelope is represented by samples. The higher the frequency of the samples, the more accurate the representation as the waveform can't change as much between samples. The higher the bits per sample, more possible values for the sample, thus reducing errors caused by moving the value of the sample to the nearest one.

9 (a) Integer, no decimal parts to store.
  (b) Real, large numbers, large range needed, but accuracy not required.
  (c) Double precision real, range and accuracy needed.
  (d) Binary coded decimal, accuracy paramount, speed not a consideration.

10 The bitmap contains information on the colour of each pixel on the screen. The vector file contains information on the co-ordinates for the centre of the circle, its diameter and its colour.

Core topic 13 Relational databases

1 The data is independent of the program accessing it, so you can add fields to the database without having to rewrite the programs that access it.

2 In a video shop loans file:

<u>001</u>, smith, fred, 01/01/72, WA3 7QD, Star Wars, 032, 100, 2, WHSMITH, 01/01/97, 03/01/97

<u>001</u>, smith, fred, 01/01/72, WA3 7QD, Empire, 034, 100, 2, WHSMITH, 04/01/97, 06/03/97

<u>001</u>, smith, fred, 01/01/72, WA3 7QD, Jedi, 037, 100, 2, WHSMITH, 07/03/97, 11/03/97

3 In a program oriented system, a program is written that says what data is to be stored and how it is to be stored. If other fields of information need to be added at a later date, then all the programs have to be altered. In a data oriented file system such as a DBMS, you only have to say what you want to store, not how.

4 The co-ordination of who's allowed to see what, what is kept in the database (upkeep of the data dictionary), users etc. is done by a database administrator.

S/he has responsibility for the database, its structure, contents and security (against both accidental and deliberate corruption). S/he must also monitor the performance of the database and reorganise it if necessary.

5 With order number as key, only one instance of a particular order number can appear in the table, so if an order concerns more than one stock item, it cannot be recorded in the table. A new table, order details, with key order number and stock item should be created.

6 See Figure 18, page 50.

Book — is written by → Authors of books ← is — Author

7 One book can have many authors, one author can write many books, so we need a linking entity.

8 A check on each non-key column in a table to see if it depends on all of a compound key or only part of it.

9 The use of users and groups with passwords and level of access to objects in the database. In a medical situation, a receptionist might see a patient's name and address and be able to alter it, but not be able to see their medical history. The doctor could see name and address and not change it, but could add to medical history.

10 A lookup function that stops incorrect data being entered, e.g. when an attempt is made to enter a loan of video a001, the database can lookup the Video table to see if there is a video with a key of a001, if not the entry is rejected.

11 To reduce data duplication and control data redundancy in a relational database.

Core topic 14 Verification/validation

1 The validation of data is done by computer programs to check that the data being input is sensible. Data verification is the process of ensuring that data has been transcribed correctly. Data can be transcribed correctly but still be nonsense.

2 The integrity of data is its correctness. It can be affected by, amongst other things, the age of the data.

3 Range check – to see whether a numeric data item lies within a given range, e.g. > 1 and <=100. Length check – to see whether a data item is too long. Presence check – to make sure a data field has not been left blank.

4 These checks are to ensure the data has not become corrupted during transmission. An example would be a parity check when the total number of ones in a character are made even (or odd), to be checked again on receipt.

5 It's a mistake made when typing when letters are juxtaposed. Verification by retyping and comparing versions avoids a large proportion of these type of errors.

6 When a long code is to be used, e.g. customer code of 15 numbers, an extra number is added to the end, found by doing a calculation on these 15 numbers. When the 16 digits are later keyed in, the computer performs the same calculation on the first 15 and if it doesn't get the 16th, then a keying-in error has occurred.

7 An error made in transcribing information from a source, e.g. misreading. Use verification or check digits.

Core topic 15 Data, information and knowledge

1 Data is the raw values relating to facts, events or transactions, e.g. data recorded when buying a tin of beans. Information is processed data, e.g. the data concerning sales is processed to produce statistical information such as total value of today's sales. Knowledge is the use of information in context; e.g. knowing today's sales of beans and sales trends I can predict how many will be sold tomorrow.

2 If data is read to 1 decimal place but an average is given to 10 places, then the coarseness of the data has reduced the quality of the information.

3 Data can age, thus old data should be updated or archived. With no date stamps old data might accidentally overwrite newer data.

4 If information like colour is encoded into data like R Y B etc., mistakes can be made later if the code is lost or misinterpreted e.g. red yellow blue/black.

5 Nature – data can be quantitative, i.e. measured, e.g. height; qualitative, i.e. a judgement about something, e.g. tall, formal, informal.

   Time – data can concern historical events, current events or future predictions.

   Frequency – this concerns how often data is captured. Data can be gathered in real-time, e.g. controlling a power station, hourly, e.g. temperature readings or other data logging, or even daily/monthly, e.g. time sheets.

   Form – data can be written, visual, e.g. pictures and graphs, aural, e.g. speech, sensory, i.e. taken from sensors, e.g. temperature.

6 Irrelevant, inaccurate, incorrect, incomplete, or delivered to the wrong person at the wrong time in the wrong amount of detail, or incomprehensible!

Extension topic 8 Information

1 Each type of information for relation to end-user **must be different**. You can use other examples, but **show the different levels**.
   - class teacher: e.g. class list showing attendance at each session over a period of time; **operational information** to resolve individual reasons for absence (i.e. a log of excuses); e.g. class pattern of absences
   - pastoral manager: e.g. individual student attendance profile reconciled against all classes for student; **tactical information** to address patterns of absence
   - senior management: e.g. monthly percentage attendance for "faculty" or school; **strategic information** to inform management decisions.

Core topic 16 Effective presentation

1 Language used should be appropriate to age group, as should the use of pictures. The AGM would most probably include graphical presentations and tables of figures not found in former.

2 The use of sound, graphics and video clips.

3 The language used was incorrect for the audience, e.g. too technical, or perhaps not technical enough.

Extension topic 10 Organisational structure

1 The links between the levels of management and their responsibilities. For example in the college diagram (on page 62) the Head of Department is responsible to the Vice Principal for any decision that is taken and the Vice Principal is ultimately responsible to the Principal. Heads of department will be responsible for the actions of the staff in their respective departments.

2 If the chain of command is vertical, as in the college structure, then the communication

system is fairly straightforward. Information tends to get passed down the chain and responses back up. The time which all this takes will depend on the length of the chain and relative efficiencies of various heads of department in informing their staff. A broad flat structure will mean that communications have to go not only across but also up the chain to the chief executive. Perhaps a central "pooling" of common information might be helpful.

3 The direction of flow of information can be fairly tightly controlled in that the flow tends to be from the senior management and back again. Decision-making is fairly easy with a limited number in the team. However, with a limited number, decision-making might be slowed down if the senior managers are not present. A wider management structure allows more staff involvement and possibly improved motivation as junior managers have more responsibility.

4 The choice could depend on the size and market position of the business. A small partnership would have all the management functions divided between the partners. A large national public company would require a wider management base in order to make use of specialist management skills.

5 Unless the changeover is treated sympathetically then such changes are a recipe for disaster as the new command structure will lead to confusion. A wider communications network might be required to allow the new groupings to keep in touch – possibly the development of an intranet or e-mail system would help.
   More teams would add to the need to distribute information more widely. More emphasis for the individual to keep in touch rather than the team leader to keep everyone informed. More home-based working might result from the growth in smaller project teams.

Extension topic 11 Information systems and organisations

1 **Operational**, the data generated by the day-to-day running of the business, processed to yield **tactical** information for middle managers to make decisions, then fed with other external information to the **strategic** level where top management make strategic decisions supported by this information.

2 Data processing is where data is captured and turned into information which forms part of a complete system. Data processing could be a self-contained, repetitive, low-level operation such as producing payslips, the results of which don't get beyond the recipients. An information system includes all means – voice, paper memoranda, written reports and electronically gathered intelligence – of providing relevant information about a business's performance on which management might make informed decisions.

3 If the information produced is taken further and becomes part of a management report or the data produced is used for management planning. For example: a payroll system will include data about employee sickness periods. This data could be extracted and compared across a number of years – useful for manpower planning.

4 Decisions are taken by managers based on the best available and convenient information. A management information system can help with the collection and analysis of data and offer a manager some possible outcomes for decisions, but the final choice is the manager's, not a computer's.

Extension topic 12 Definition of a management information system

1 a) Purpose: to convert data from internal and external sources into information.
  b) Why required: to enable managers to make effective decisions, or information can be produced from a large quantity of data in a selective manner quickly.
  c) Example: any acceptable example but it must be related to management decision-making, e.g. in a nation-wide distribution company the use of an MIS to monitor the movement of vehicles and revise strategic planning of the location of warehouses.

Notice this emphasis on internal and external sources.

Reading the weekly computer press would help with examples.

Extension topic 13 The development and life cycle of an information system

1 Advantages: forces the management team to think in a logical manner and to plan ahead; introduces the principle of system appraisal in line with business needs; phased

ANSWERS 121

introduction of system; prototyping help to trace errors/faults in system; user involvement with the development process; higher degree of user acceptability and successful running of system. Disadvantages: might be too formal and inflexible – difficult to cope with specification changes; may take too long to go through all the stages; delay might cause budget over-run.

2 A logical sequence is offered from problem analysis to system specification and design. Time sequence is offered which allows changeovers to be managed as part of the project. Budgetary control can be maintained as commitments are identified. Future developments – upgrade paths for hardware/software can be part of the overall cycle.

Extension topic 14 Success or failure of a management information system

1 See the points listed on page 69 and **think positive** – for example to have professional standards, to keep records and to operate as a team.

2 An IT champion is someone who is enthusiastic for the technology, can recognise how individual or departmental productivity could be increased and is persuasive about what can be achieved. Needed because of reluctance to use IT on part of other employees, because they can't recognise the benefits. Those with limited skills may require encouragement to use technology.

3 Management may not fully appreciate the benefits obtainable from IT. Managers need to see the necessity of planning IT developments in a similar manner to other parts of the business. The development of an IT strategy could help manage the future costs of hardare/software. Senior management are responsible for authorising and paying for changes – they ought to appreciate what they are paying for.

Extension topic 15 Information flow

1 Relevant, timely, to the right person, through the correct channels and in a presentation format appropriate for its purpose.

2 Poor flow means the correct information is not getting through the system. It is likely to be incomplete and dated, therefore decisions taken in good faith lead to poor business performance.

3 Inspection of current I/O sub-systems. Observation of current I/O sub-systems. Tracking of documents for input. Tracking of documents for output. Inspection of development requests. Inspection of report/information requests. Interviews with end-users. Questionnaires (at any level as above).

Extension topic 16 Personnel and information systems

1 Your answer should include:
   (a) Factors influencing information flow: Organisation structure: the number of levels through which information must flow. Geographical structure of the organisation: distributed. How data originates within an organisation. Where data originates within an organisation. The validity of data (re-collection affects quality of information). The preparation and input of data (including timing). The volume of data to be collected and input. The processing cycle. The specification of reports. The report distribution cycle. The report timing cycle. Formal vs informal requests and responses. Quality of data. The techniques/structure for monitoring and organising the information flow.

   (b) Techniques: Inspection of current I/O sub-systems. Observation of current I/O sub-systems. Tracking of documents for input. Tracking of documents for output. Inspection of development requests. Inspection of report/information requests. Interviews with end-users. Questionnaires (at any level as above).

Candidates should distinguish between data and information

We are looking for HOW these things might be done

Extension topic 17 Developments within management information systems

1 Ease of use, fast response, ability to generate graphical output, built on (usually) relational database systems accessed indirectly through a query language, access to the corporate databases. Benefits: before the actual decision is made: ability to handle a large amount

of data in a short period; ability try out different decisions and to review results; ability to share different possibilities with other senior managers.

2 Depends upon the context of use – it is valid for all levels of management – operational, tactical and strategic – but is likely to be in decision support because of the "What if?" questions which can be built in.

3 Word-processing, spreadsheet, database and scheduling software.

4 Software which provides tools to help the user schedule tasks, manage resources, monitor costs and generate reports for analysis and presentation.

Extension topic 18 Corporate information systems strategy

1 Management organisation and functions; planning and decision making methods; general organisation structure; responsibility for the information system within an organisation; information flow; hardware and software; behavioural factors, e.g. personalities, motivation, ability to adapt to change.

2 Plans the use of IT resources. Helps the company to cope with change or disasters. Company can maintain a consistent approach towards hardware/software purchases and upgrades. Consideration given to staff training needs.

How to prepare strategy: Assessment of what IT resources the company already owns; assessment of how these resources are used; assessment of how they might be used in future; recognition of the need to protect the company's investment in resources – data, equipment and human.

Extension topic 19 Expert systems and artificial intelligence

1 A type of problem-solving model, almost always implemented on a computer, that deals with a problem the way an 'expert' does – such as doctor or lawyer. The solution process involves consulting a base of knowledge or expertise to reason out an answer based on the characteristics of the problem. See page 80 for the example of Apache III.

2 It should allow a user to solve a problem; explain to the user, to some extent, how it solved that problem and provide a reliable means of solving similar problems. Circumstances could include: the planning of a new manufacturing process, the pricing and market positioning of a new product, or investment appraisal for a new shopping complex or manufacturing plant.

3 Assumption that the knowledge base of the system is up-to-date and is relevant to the type of decision to be taken. Many business decisions are about management 'feelings' for a market – an 'instinct' for what is going to happen. This is unlikely to be part of an expert system. Decision-making could become too 'mechanistic' without considering the human resource implications of the decision.

Core topic 17 Capabilities and limitations of IT systems

1 Volume: large amount of data is being stored/retrieved and updated (1 filing cabinet = 1 CD-ROM). Accuracy: the processing requires accuracy. Repetition: data is to be processed in a repetitive manner.

2 A major bank wanted to introduce a cheque scanning system that would scan a cheque, do optical character recognition and store the resulting scan. On doing the sums it was found to take too long as it would have taken 30 hours to process one day's cheques.

3 A limit on number of fields in a database, a limit on concurrent users to a shared database, a limit on length of filename.

4 The system had small volumes of data, with little processing activity and searching, e.g. small card index.

Extension topic 20 The management of change

1. Possible answers might include: attitude of management and workforce resentment; skill levels and re-skilling; structure of organisation and key roles = restructuring = job loss; conditions of service = legislation; internal procedures for operations; external image; culture of organisation = style.

Extension topic 21 Audit requirements

1. Audit – checking that things, people and systems are where they should be and doing what they should be doing. Audit trail – if files have been used then an indication – note or reference – should be placed on the file to indicate any additions/subtractions from the file and where supporting documents can be found.

2. It is not good practice to have those making claims on a company – for example for travelling expenses – also being responsible for settling the claims – opportunity for fraud.

3. Companies have legal obligations to – for example – manage their finances in a clear and open manner and to keep data secure under the terms of the Data Protection Act 1984. As part of this obligation, evidence needs to support reasons why changes have been made and those responsible for making the changes need to do it in a careful and easily followed manner.

4. Any from the following: when was the file accessed; where was it accessed – local or remote site; by whom was it accessed; what action was taken on the file – additions/deletions; what copies were produced – soft or hard copies; where were the copies deposited; when was the file closed.

Extension topic 22 Disaster recovery management

1. A procedure which says what steps a company must take when IT equipment fails leading to a complete loss of processing facilities and data. A company might have a considerable investment in both data and equipment, which generates income for the company. Systems failure could result in heavy losses for the company. An efficient and effective recovery procedure is therefore essential.

2. See contents of Extension topic 22 for guidance as to possible report content.

Core topic 18 Security, the Data Protection Act and EU Directives

1. Protection against physical loss or damage; protection against unauthorised copying; protection against unauthorised viewing; protection against unauthorised amendment.

2. Valuable information could pass to a business competitor. The data is a major, valuable company asset. The company is bound by the terms of Data Protection Act 1984.

3. See page 93.

4. See contents of Core topic 18 and Extension topic 23 for guidance.

5. Breaches of the Data Protection Act 1984. Considerable financial penalties due to loss of working data. Possible bankruptcy.

Extension topic 23 Legal aspects

1. See the contents of Extension topic 23, page 97.

2. See the contents of Extension topic 23, page 97.

3. Companies don't wish to look foolish or incompetent in the eyes of customers and business partners, might lead to withdrawal of custom and loss of income. Discussion of security problems might lead others to attempt to gain unauthorised access. Prosecution of employees could lead to further, open disclosures of security weaknesses.

Core topic 19 IT and the professional

1 The BCS has produced a comprehensive set of standards for the training and development of all those working in information systems and related fields.

This is called the industry structure model (ISM) and it defines many different functions in information systems – including programmers, software engineers, network specialists and hybrid managers – at ten levels of responsibility and technical expertise. The ISM allows your current job description to show where you lie in the model, and which paths are open to you and the training required for these paths.

> *Reasons for choice are important at A level. Get beyond description!*

2 A code of practice is not a legal document, just a declaration of intent. The company wants to promote a quality image above and beyond legal requirements to boost customer confidence.

3 The customer is aware from the code of practice that the company intends to give a certain level of service beyond what is required by law.

4 The industry structure model (ISM) defines many different functions in information systems – including programmers, software engineers, network specialists and hybrid managers – at ten levels of responsibility and technical expertise. It was developed to help employees and employers determine training needs and salary levels.

5 Good communication skills, ability to work in a team, high level of IT skills, good project management skills.

6 By identifying the functions of the job in IT terms, and the level of technical expertise and responsibility, these made be mapped on the model to determine salary.

Extension topic 24 Training

1 For supported self study where the user wishes to learn at his/her own pace.

2 As developments in IT systems occur personnel must be trained in the updated systems in parallel with these developments, otherwise staff would not be able to function efficiently when the newer versions are introduced.

3 Texts containing 'what's new' information, followed by hands-on tutorial sessions, backed up by interactive video training systems/refreshers as required.

4 Interaction allows for prompts and demos as further help. More user choice and ability to score performance, i.e. management feedback, and user can see improvements made.

Extension topic 25 User support

1 See list on page 103 for guidance.

2 Growth in the market for IT equipment, both business and domestic. More powerful equipment allows for more built-in help facilities. Growing non-expert use of IT equipment, therefore more help required. User expectations have increased as to the help which ought to be available.

3 How to: get started/enter text/number/save file/print file/close down/reminder about backing up files.

How to: get saved or backed-up files/edit current files – adding or deleting text/close down/reminder about backing up files.

How to: insert graphics and tables/edit graphics and tables/links to other applications (e.g. Word documents to RTF (Rich Text Format) or Excel tables to Dbase format)/reminder about backing up and archiving files.

4 Information technology is a practical 'hands-on' actitivy. Users like to investigate on their own how to use a system. Reading manuals is sometimes seen as an admission of defeat. However, more advanced features cannot be learnt without access to manuals in order to

check out the examples. Software designers could add on-line help facilities, give practical demonstrations of how features work, build in 'cue cards' – step-by-step prompts to help set up a feature. All the support could be contained within the package once loaded.

A major drawback is the large amount of extra storage required for the on-line help – sometimes more than the application!

Core topic 20 Role of IT and its social impact

1. IT system used to monitor and inform of a patient's condition; if it failed, it could be catastrophic for the individual concerned as the necessary alarm is not sounded.

   IT system used to control a nuclear power station could fail and result in meltdown as in 3 Mile Island or Chernobyl. The result would not only be a catastrophe for the organisation but for a large number of the population.

2. Teleconferencing means holding a conference or meeting at a distance and employs the use of a wide area network and the use of small cameras, microphones and loudspeakers, to broadcast the sound and image to one or more recipients. It enables remote sites to communicate.

3. Organisations whose core business will not be affected by the introduction of the Internet but whose business will be extended should take advantage of this outlet. For example, a mail order business that sells plastic-ware with interests in catalogue shopping will find that a move to Internet shopping has a small customer base, as their traditional customers are not likely to have access to the required equipment.

   A company that sells direct through computers is more likely to succeed as the customer base in the Internet is large and computer-friendly and also, the use of the Internet will extend its range of activities, not simply divert from one method to another.

   Banks who have direct banking facilities would advertise on the Net as the punters reading them must have access to the equipment.

   Supermarkets can offer Internet sales and delivery, good for house-bound and those with little time to shop.

   The speed of the system for browsing pictures is rather poor at the moment and an improvement in data transfer rate, either by faster land-line modems or cable modems should help this problem. There is the possibility of EFT, but the problems in no physical contact with the goods can put customers off.

   There is great customer worry about Internet security in the UK when paying by credit card, whereas in the USA, about 1% of gross domestic product is over the WWW.

   There is a potential risk in using the Net if a firewall is not in place as remote computers can possibly get into your system if this is not in place. A virus can also be transmitted when files are read or opened.

   To the company, the investment in equipment is a large one, which may be out-sourced to a third party, but it would require changes in the organisation within a company if it was to wholly move to a new system. The social impact would include the retraining of staff and the possible loss of jobs in the retail sector, but delivery sector with pick and drop would be enlarged. Instead of us travelling to the shops, the goods would come to us.

   The total number of journeys would be less and pollution would decrease.

Index

access to data 30, 91–3
artificial intelligence 79–81
audit requirements 85–7

back-up copies of data 29, 89
backbone 20
bar code reader 9
batch processing 44
bitmaps 8–9, 12
bridge 20, 23
business applications 8, 38, 64–5, 73–6
business organisation 62–3, 71, 77–8

communication methods 12, 18–26
computer-aided applications 34–5
computer output on microfilm 10–11
configurability of hard/software 42–3
corporate information systems 77–8
   security 97–8
corruption of data 29–31, 93

data 55, 58–9
   corruption 29–31, 93
   handling 27–8, 47–55, 64, 66
   processing 45, 64
   quality 52–4, 56–7, 66, 71
   safe keeping 29–31, 88–98
databases 23, 47–51
decision support systems 64–6, 73–6
disaster recovery management 88–90
distributed systems 23
drivers 42–3

education 107, 109
e-fax 25
e-mail 22, 25
encryption 30, 92
entity relationship diagram 49–50
executive information systems 75–6
expert systems 55–6, 79–81
export filter 27

facilities management 105–6
fax 25
file server 19–20, 89–90
fuzzy logic 80–1

geographical information systems 33–4

hackers 29–30
hardware 5–6
   configurability 42–3
human–computer interfaces 13–17, 74–5

import filter 27
informatics 21, 25
information 55–60, 66
information systems in organisations
      64–6, 74–81
   development 67–8, 83–4
   impact 109–10
   personnel 73
   security 91–8
   success or failure 69, 88–90
information technology
   professionals and training 99–102
   role and social impact 107–11
   teams 105
input devices 8
intelligent systems 79–81
interactive processing 44
internet super highway 21–2

knowledge base 55–6, 79–80

leisure applications 107
local area networks 18–19, 22

magnetic ink character reader 9, 55
management information systems 64–6,
      73–8, 83–4
   success or failure 69–70, 88–90
managing change 83–4
mathematical packages 35
modems 21–2
music applications 35

network speeds 22
networks 18–23
normalisation of data 47–9
numbers 45

open system inter-connection model
      20–1, 23
optical character recognition 8–9, 12
optical mark reader 9
organisation
   information flow 64–5, 71–2, 109–10
   structure 62–3, 77–8, 105–6
output devices 9–11

packet switching systems 25–6
passwords 30, 92
peripherals 8–12, 42–3
personnel information systems 73
pictures 45, 61
plotter 10

plug and play systems 42
portability of data 27–8
power loss 89–90
presentations 61
printers 9–10
privacy 93–6
problem–solving systems 79–80
processing 44–6, 64
project management 34, 105–6
public services and information
    technology 107–10

real-time processing 44
recovery strategy 89–90
relational databases 47–51, 75
repeaters 20, 23

security 88, 91–8
  legal aspects 97–8
social effects of technology 107–11
software
  applications 5–7, 33–7, 107–10
  business 73–6, 79–82
  capabilities 32–7, 82
  configurability 42–3

reliability and testing 40–1

sound output 11
sound processing 45–6
speech input/output 9, 15
statistical packages 35
storage devices 11–12

telematics 21, 25
telemessage 25
telephones 24
television 24
telex 25
text 45
transaction processing 44
transmission 18, 53–4

upgradability 38–9
user interface 6, 13–17, 74–5, 80
user support 103–4

validation and verification of data 52–4, 66
viewdata 24
virus attack 29–30

wide area networks 21–2
working practice changes 83–4, 108–9